WOMEN AS HEADTEACHERS
striking the balance

WOMEN AS HEADTEACHERS
striking the balance

Marianne Coleman

Trentham Books

Stoke on Trent, UK and Sterling, USA

Trentham Books Limited

Westview House	22883 Quicksilver Drive
734 London Road	Sterling
Oakhill	VA 20166-2012
Stoke on Trent	USA
Staffordshire	
England ST4 5NP	

First published 2002

British Library Cataloguing-in-Publication Data
A catalogue record for this book is available from the British Library

1 85856 258 9

Designed and typeset by Trentham Print Design Ltd., Chester and printed in Great Britain by Cromwell Press Ltd., Wiltshire.

Contents

Acknowledgements • vi

Introduction • vii

Chapter 1
Setting the scene • 1

Chapter 2
Building a career as headteacher: the success factors • 13

Chapter 3
Becoming a headteacher • 35

Chapter 4
Career and family: Can there be a balance? • 49

Chapter 5
Relationships with partners: partners and children
in career planning • 63

Chapter 6
Stereotypes: macho leadership or niceness and tears? • 79

Chapter 7
Exploding the myth of the masculine leader • 97

Chapter 8
Being a woman headteacher: constraints,
problems and liberation • 121

Chapter 9
Do headteachers promote the career
development of women? • 139

Chapter 10
Conclusions: women in headship –
striking a balance • 149

References • 163

Appendix • 171

Acknowledgements

I should like to thank all my friends and colleagues at the Educational Management Development Unit (now Centre for Educational Leadership and Management) of the University of Leicester for all their help and support in the writing of this book and during the work that led up to it. My particular thanks to Jacky Lumby for all her encouragement, Ann Briggs for keeping me going to the end, Tony Bush who gave me so many opportunities and helped me take them up, Pip Murray and Joyce Palmer who have provided such willing support for many years and Rob Dixon for his help with statistical analysis. I should also like to thank Gillian Klein of Trentham Books for her painstaking editing and encouragement. I owe a debt of gratitude to the late Valerie Hall whose work is quoted at length in this book and who was an example and inspiration to me.

The book would not have been written without the constant support of my family, John, Daniel and David who have helped me to find my particular balance in life.

Finally I acknowledge the debt I owe to all the headteachers, women and men, who were kind enough to participate in my research.

Introduction

L eadership in all walks of life is generally identified with men. Although most teachers are women, in schools in the UK and elsewhere, the overwhelming majority of headteachers are men – only about a quarter of the secondary heads in England and Wales are women. This book is based on the views of the women and men who are headteachers and is addressed to the people who are concerned with the management of our schools, especially those who wish to become headteachers. The subtitle refers to the apparent imbalance that exists in our society with regard to gender and management. It also refers to the difficulties in striking a balance between home and paid work. I hope therefore that the book will be read by men as well as women. The issues of equity and of school management, and the personal dilemmas of managing home and paid work, affect both men and women.

When I was developing the ideas for the book I identified a number of the underlying questions that might be asked by women who aspire to management and leadership in schools and which could be at least partially answered by the data I had gathered from two large surveys of headteachers in England and Wales. These questions were:

- How can I make it to the top? What can be learned from the experience of today's headteachers?

- Who is likely to offer help and support on the way?

- Will I be able to manage being a parent and having a career?

- Are we living in a changing world where men and women are increasingly regarded as equal in terms of work and family?

- Will I be up against institutionalised views that make my career progress difficult?

- Will I have credibility as a leader and manager if I combine motherhood and a career?

- How will men react to being managed by a woman?
- Will I have to be seen to lead like a man if I am going to be considered a good headteacher?
- What is it like being a woman headteacher?

A number of issues and questions also emerged for the headteachers themselves about how they might be encouraging gender equity in school management:

- What career support and advice are we offering?
- Do we provide career mentoring?
- Are we offering appropriate role models?
- How do we view maternity leave?
- Are we family friendly?
- Are we aware of sexist behaviour?
- Are we feminists?

The answers to the questions came from two surveys. The first was of all the women headteachers in England and Wales in the late 1990s, followed by a second survey of the same number of men headteachers. In addition I had already carried out in-depth interviews with a number of women heads. Data from the interviews are used in this book but the main source of data is the two surveys. These brought responses from close to 1,000 secondary headteachers and allowed me to draw comparisons between the career paths and the views of the men and women heads on their roles and the part played in their lives by work and family. The outcomes offer food for thought on the issues listed above.

Chapter One sets the scene for the book in terms of the present imbalance relating to leadership and gender in both practical and theoretical terms. Chapters Two and Three trace the course of building a career towards headship for both women and men, while Chapters Four and Five consider the difficulties of balancing work and family. Chapters Six, Seven and Eight look at how the headteachers operate and what it is actually like to be a woman headteacher. Chapter Nine shows what headteachers do and could do in terms of promoting the career development of women and Chapter Ten offers some conclusions about the issues of balance in work and the family.

1
Setting the scene

- How can I make it to the top? What can be learned from the experience of today's headteachers?

This book is about the secondary headteachers of England and Wales. Its focus is gender and how this relates to becoming and being a headteacher. The initial impetus for the research came from my realisation that, despite the fact that half the teachers in secondary schools are women, a relatively small proportion actually become headteachers (see table 1.1 below). This disproportion of female managers and leaders is typical of the gender balance that exists in management as a whole, both in this country and internationally.

Since the subjects of the book are secondary headteachers in England and Wales who have the task of leading and managing schools, the main context for discussion of their work is inevitably the world of education. However, questions about the ways in which women and men lead and manage and questions about differences in their styles apply both internationally and to all aspects of paid employment, and it is certainly relevant to look beyond the UK and beyond the school at wider studies of how gender affects management and leadership behaviour. Taking the experience of headteachers and looking at the ways in which gender relates to their work and their family life therefore has relevance to wider groups of managers. The questions I consider in this book apply to all women and men balancing career and family choices. They are also relevant to social attitudes and the wider structures of society. I have drawn insights from international research, and research on management in general.

The gender of leaders in education

Despite the importance of gender in all our lives, it is surprisingly difficult to obtain official statistics in most countries that separate women and men in the management of education. Consequently some of the statistics that follow may seem a little out of date, as in some cases they have been obtained from secondary sources, or the relevant government may not publish statistics on a regular basis.

Women numerically dominate the teaching profession in most countries, (DfEE, 2000a; Shakeshaft, 1989; Blackmore, 1989; Davies, 1990), but they hold a minority of the management positions in education, apart from schools which cater for very young children, which are more often managed by women. Women teachers in junior, middle and secondary schools and in colleges and universities are less likely to achieve management positions than their male peers and the older the age group of students the less likely this becomes.

In the secondary sector in the UK, the proportions of women and men teachers are roughly equal but the positions that are better paid and involve greater levels of management responsibility are more likely to be held by men. Men are more than three times as likely to achieve secondary headship than their female peers. Approximately 3.6 per cent of male teachers achieve headship but the same is true for only one per cent of female teachers. The most recent figures currently available (DfEE, 2000a) show a gradual but steady increase in the percentage of female heads and deputy heads between 1992 and 1999. However, the equal opportunities legislation that has been in place since the 1970s has not resulted in radical change.

These figures also hide discrepancies between regions. Wales has fewer than the average numbers of female heads at both primary and secondary level. Yewlett (1996) comments on the traditional attitudes towards women in educational management in Wales, particularly in the industrial areas of south Wales. Welsh Office statistics (1995) show that only eight per cent of the 237 secondary schools in Wales have female headteachers and that this is true for 43 per cent of the primary schools. Darling and Glendinning (1996) report on gender inequities in the distribution of promoted posts in Scotland. The most recent figures (ONS, 2001) give a total of six per cent of heads and deputy heads as female in Scottish secondary schools.

Table 1.1: Percentage of full-time teachers in maintained secondary schools in England and Wales 1992 - 1999 by grade and sex

	Heads		Deputies		Classroom and other teachers	
Year	men	women	men	women	men	women
1992	78.1	21.9	66.1	33.9	49.1	50.9
1993	78.1	21.9	66.3	33.7	48.6	51.4
1994	78.0	22.0	66.0	34.0	48.1	51.9
1995	76.4	23.6	66.1	33.9	47.5	52.5
1996	75.8	24.2	65.5	34.5	47.0	53.0
1997	75.1	24.9	65.1	34.9	46.4	53.6
1998	73.1	26.9	64.9	35.1	47.0	53.0
1999	72.1	27.9	63.8	36.2	45.3	54.7
(DfEE 2000a)						

Edwards and Lyons (1994) identified considerable differences in England and Wales in the proportion of female secondary heads appointed. Whilst London boroughs appoint female headteachers almost as often as male heads, the shire counties as a whole have an average of 13 per cent of female heads. At the time of their research in 1992, there was not a single woman head in Northumberland and Dyfed, and County Durham had women in only two per cent of its headships.

Women are well represented as staff of further education colleges but constitute only 17 per cent of the principals (Stott and Lawson, 1997). However, this represents a change in favour of women, since in 1990 there were only 13 female principals of FE colleges, and by 1996 there were 68 (*ibid.*). The overall proportion of women in the universities is relatively low. In 1999-2000, 30 per cent of all university academic staff but only twelve per cent of professors were women (HESA, 2000).

The relatively small proportion of women in senior management positions in education should be seen in the wider context of the proportion of women who obtain management positions in the UK in general. A national management survey indicated that only 3.6 per cent of all directors in the UK were women in 1998 (Vinnicombe, 2000). Over 70 per cent of women between the ages of 25 and 59 are classified as economically active (ONS, 2001) but most of them are in specific employment areas in the tertiary sector and in support and 'caring' roles. High proportions of women work in public administration, education and health but numerical dominance does not bring about a major share of top management positions in the professions associated with women. For example, in nursing women form a disproportionately small part of the management echelon. A report for the Equal Opportunities Commission in Northern Ireland (Morgan, *et al*, 1995) identified that 32.3 per cent of male nurses were managers compared to 10.5 per cent of female nurses. Approximately equal numbers of men and women enter publishing, but men are twice as likely as women to become managers (Walsh and Cassell, 1995).

Women in educational management are in a minority in the UK. They are also in a minority in most other countries, whatever the level of development.

In the USA, senior management in schools is located in the super-intendency, with an overview of the school district, and in the principal-ship of high schools, where there might be several in a district. 1990 figures show that, over the country as a whole, women constituted 4.6 per cent of the superintendents and 17.3 per cent of the assistant super-intendents, whilst 20.6 per cent of high school principals were women (American Association of School Administrators, 1992).

In New Zealand secondary schools, 51 per cent of teachers are female but 81 per cent of the principals are male (Pringle and Timperley, 1995). In Australia, the encouragement of women through affirmative action has led to 'an incremental increase in female principals' (Blackmore, 1994, p.2). However, Blackmore claims that this has been accompanied by a subtle change in the locus of power towards mainly male administrators outside the schools making 'the decisions at the 'core'' (*ibid.*), a situation she compares to Israel (Goldring and Chen, 1994), where women are in the majority as secondary principals but the more powerful administrators outside the schools are almost exclusively male. Singapore too, has a relatively high proportion of female secondary heads – 53 per cent of the total (Morris *et al* 1999).

In the rest of Europe, as in the UK, female headteachers or principals of secondary level schools are in the minority. The position in Ireland is complicated by the existence of three different types of schools at secondary levels each with its own traditions and administrative structures (Lynch, 1997). However, 29 per cent of all 782 school principals at secondary level are women (*ibid.*). The figure is slightly higher than that for the UK and is likely to be connected to the relatively large proportion of single sex schools in Eire (Ruijs, 1993). The relative prevalence of girls' schools in the UK and Ireland helps to maintain the proportion of female heads in comparison to the Netherlands, for example, where Ruijs (1993) comments on the reduction in the numbers of female heads over the last twenty to thirty years as a result of the virtual disappearance of single sex schools. Figures for the Netherlands show that in 1995-6 women constituted 33 per cent of teachers in secondary schools, 12 per cent of deputy heads and seven per cent of heads (Vermeulen and Ruijs, 1997).

Figures on the gender of headteachers have not been collected in Spain for some time; the most recent figures available are for 1985 when 20 per cent of secondary heads were female (Santos, 1997). In France, 56 per cent of secondary teachers and 30 per cent of secondary headteachers are women (Fave-Bonnet, 1997). In Germany it appears that women are poorly represented in school management. 'In the case of the *Gymnasien*: these are firmly in the hands of men; female heads are the absolute exception' (Faulstich-Wieland, 1997, p.62).

In a wide-ranging review of teaching staff in countries in Africa, Central America, India and China, Davies (1990) concluded:

> Whether or not therefore the profession is female dominated numerically, formal decision-making is in the hands of men. ... Educational administration is still seen as a masculine occupation in many countries. (p.62)

In China, obtaining official national or provincial statistics is difficult but when I was involved in research in the north-west Shaanxi province (Coleman *et al* 1998) the numbers of women represented in senior management teams in that area was very small, particularly in secondary education in urban areas, and in all schools in the rural areas. Statistics are also difficult to collect in African countries. Pre the first democratic elections in South Africa women made up 43 per cent of the secondary level teaching force but 90 per cent of principals were male (Kotecha, 1994).

So the context of this book is an educational pattern in which women are generally less likely than men to be headteachers of secondary schools and where the expectation is that the leader will be male.

The research for this book

My initial starting point of surprise at the relatively small number of women headteachers led me to a review of the literature in educational management of sources relating to women's management and leadership and then to the investigation of two specific questions which underlie the research project:

- What are the barriers to the progress of women?

- Do women manage and lead differently to men?

The more detailed questions I went on to ask were all based on areas that had been identified through the literature as being relevant to these two main questions (Coleman, 1994). The interview schedule and questionnaire developed are in appendix 1. Interviews with a small number of women headteachers and a survey of all the secondary women headteachers in England and Wales were undertaken in the latter half of the 1990s, and these have been reported separately (Coleman, 1996a, 1996b). Although there is an increasing amount of research that considers female as well as male managers in school, as Hall (1993) points out in Britain, 'overall the research is mainly descriptive and based on small samples' (p.25).

The data from a survey offered an opportunity to catch a glimpse, a snapshot, of the opinions of the headteachers at the end of the twentieth century. A large survey is a fairly unusual research instrument to use in connection with gender issues, since feminist research has tended to reject quantitative methods, which are seen as part of positivist 'patriarchal dominance' (Atkinson *et al*, 1993, p.25). Feminist methodology is more often identified within the qualitative, interpretive, phenomenological research approach. For example, Adler *et al* (1993), when interviewing 44 women in education, declare that:

> ...our sample was not representative in any way, nor did we try to generalize about women's experience from the data we obtained. Rather, we resisted accepting either of these ideas as meaningful. The research project itself and qualitative methods we used reflected our subjective approach. (p.63)

Usher (1996) regards feminism as a 'perspective' rather than a methodology that can inform the use of both quantitative and qualitative methods. Rejecting the essentialist approach to women, Usher (1996) states that:

> Feminist theory now uses the full range of methods and immerses itself in the greatest range of subject matters, challenging the false homogeneity of much that passes for understanding of the social world. (p.131)

My book is written from a feminist point of view in that it takes the influence of gender on lives and leadership as the key theme. It is unusual because the research is based primarily on questions that were initially asked of women about their lives and experience in leadership. The picture seemed incomplete without asking men headteachers the same questions so I undertook a survey of a one in four sample of male headteachers. This meant that I asked questions of 670 women (the total number of women secondary heads) and 670 men (a random sample of the men).

The starting point for all the questioning was the issues that had been raised through the literature about women in management, especially educational management. The subjects covered in the survey were very different from research that simply looked at the role of headteacher or their management style. Perhaps it was this difference that encouraged the majority of the headteachers to participate in the survey. Over 70 per cent of the women and later, over 60 per cent of the men, responded. The high response rate of the women was partially explained in the numerous comments and letters that accompanied the returning questionnaires. These showed that many of the women had welcomed the opportunity to consider and respond to questions that were obviously close to their hearts. Some thanked me for asking the questions and clearly welcomed the opportunity of commenting on their position as women headteachers. The relatively high response rate of the men was extremely pleasing in view of the fact that the questions had been derived from literature highlighting issues that related particularly to women. The letter accompanying the questionnaire to the men mentioned the high response rate by the women and this may have spurred them on. The questions seemed to capture the interest of the majority of headteachers, both female and male.

Gender issues are usually seen as women's issues. However, there is now a growing body of work that considers the conceptualisation of male gender and the impact on life and life choices. There is also a popular awareness of the long hours worked in the UK and elsewhere, and the impact on our family lives and the quality of our lives generally (DfEE, 2000b). It may be that these underlying trends encouraged some of the responses. The main focus of this book is the experience of women as headteachers, the challenges that they face as headteachers both in their paid work and in finding a balance between work and home. Men also face these issues although there is generally less pressure on them in respect of home responsibilities.

The subtitle of this book refers to 'striking a balance' and this provides the leitmotiv for the book as whole. A balance is to be found in many ways: in terms of individuals' life choices and in the ways they manage their personal and professional life, including their chosen management and leadership style. These issues are discussed in detail in the chapters that follow. The question of a wider balance in society also exists. The main themes of the evolution of thinking about women's and men's place in society follows as these underpin some of the major concerns of this book.

The conceptualisation of gender

Until relatively recently, gender issues were seen as women's issues and analysed accordingly. Now there is a literature that identifies issues of masculinities, as opposed to one way of viewing the masculine style of management (Collinson and Hearn, 1996; Mac an Ghaill, 1994; Kerfoot and Knights, 1995). However, gender issues have a much longer history of analysis through the different waves of feminist theory that have emerged since the 1960s. In reviewing how feminism has interpreted women and leadership, Blackmore (1999, p.52) points out that:

> A range of different theoretical and strategic positions now co-exists and overlaps within the literature on women and leadership. Each of these discursive 'positions' mobilizes different logics and gender change strategies.

The disproportion of women in leadership roles can be simply seen as a matter of equity. Liberal feminism would take a view that the 'problem' could and should be eliminated by ensuring policies of equal opportunities: 'The concern is more with equality in the sense of access and opportunity based on merit or credentials as opposed to equality of outcomes' (Bensimon and Marshall, 1997, p.4). However, this view does not take into account the distribution of power in society, it does not address the 'socially constructed meaning of gender' (Schmuck, 1996, p.350).

An alternative view is styled 'women's ways feminisms' (Marshall, 1997, p.12) or 'essentialist feminism' (Usher, 1996, p.123). This is a view of women as different and excelling in qualities associated with nurturing. This view actually celebrates women and their potential (Gilligan, 1982) and the ethics of care (Noddings, 1984). The literature showing that women operate in collaborative, caring ways leads to the logical conclusion that women operate in a different and, implicitly better way than men. This view of cultural feminism identifies 'competitive individualism, socially constructed views of merit and skill, hierarchical and authoritarian structures, aggressive and rights oriented behaviours as masculinist, and problematic' (Blackmore, 1999, p.53). However, 'all women are not all one way' (Schmuck, 1996, p.353) and neither are all men, and this view does not allow for the range of modes of operation of either sex. More importantly, this deterministic view of gender does not take into account the cultural bias which identifies qualities like caring and the traditional feminine values with a lesser status based on the rational/irrational dichotomy of John Stuart Mill, who identified rationalism as a masculine trait and at least suggests (Usher, 1996, p.122) that woman's lack of this trait may be part of her nature. The concomitant of this is that the caring and nurturing qualities tend to be relegated to the private rather than the public sphere that leaves

> ... women vulnerable and segregated, with all the caring and community duties and no recognition of the political forces defining their worth. The danger also comes from essentializing women and endowing them exclusively with these perspectives, leaving men free of relationship and caring responsibilities. (Marshall, 1997, p.12)

More radical views including Marxist and socialist feminism, postmodern and post-structuralist feminism focus on the economic and political structures of society, identifying power as being in the hands of men and that power being maintained through the family and the culture of patriarchy. This view of the influence of gender on leadership and management is diametrically opposed to that of the liberal feminists. The claim is that:

> Even if sexism was eliminated and both sexes participated fully, the patriarchal nature of structures and value systems would still ensure that men and women were placed in unequal positions of power, and that female activity was defined as marginal and of lesser significance than male experience. (Usher, 1996, p.124)

Feminism has shared with critical theory a focus on the need for change, particularly of structures. However, all aspects of feminism open up the prospect of seeing society differently. Gosetti and Rusch (1995) refer to the need to develop a feminist 'lens':

> By using a women-centred lens, contemporary feminism is able to move beyond the consideration of women as an 'add-on' issue and, instead, look at society, culture, and the world from the standpoint of being female. (p.15)

Grundy (1993) goes beyond this to develop a critique of 'emancipatory praxis' recognizing that:

> ...the way things are perceived to be may, in fact, be the way they are being made to appear so that some existing unequal relationships and unjust practices may not be recognized for what they are. (p.171)

Whilst it is important for equal opportunities policies to be in place, the cultural identification of women as caring, domestic and implicitly of lesser importance and status than men needs to be examined. The tensions are apparent in the role female leaders are playing in schools and elsewhere:

> Those women who have achieved positions that are held predominantly by men have realised, consciously or unconsciously, that there are social roles and expectations governing the role of females from the culture. They must become 'abnormal' women; they must transcend the social expectations of femaleness in order to aspire to the socially prescribed role of leader. And because they do not fit the expectations of the attributes of leaders, they are also 'abnormal' administrators. Their position as administrators makes them 'insiders' to the organisation, but their 'abnormal status as women makes them 'outsiders' in their organizations' (Schmuck, 1996, p.356).

Men too may be identified and stereotyped in ways that may not necessarily be helpful to them. Men are associated with a type of management that is 'heroic' (Collinson and Hearn, 2000, p.264) where one charismatic leader drives initiatives. Alongside these qualities, men are often associated with the concept of managerialism linked to their implicit rationalism and in opposition to the essentialist view of women as caring. The stereotyping of men has been countered by the concept of 'masculinities', allowing for a range of ways of behaving that take into account class, race and sexual orientation. However, these categories are considered to be unfixed and shifting (Collinson and Hearn, 2000, p.267).

Blackmore (1999) speaks for a re-formulation of authority that is not based on the binary divisions that have been exposed by gender theorising and advocates:

> ...a mode of reason in opposition to emotion or justice in opposition to care. Such an approach, which views emotion and reason, justice and care, as integral to each other, creates possibilities to develop feminist discourses of leadership that interrogate male/female dualisms, that offer substantive ethical positions, but that can also provide an ongoing analysis of their political effects. (p.56)

From this brief overview, crucial points emerge:

- There are a range of views, extending from those of liberal feminists working for equal opportunities, to critical feminists who would wish to change society radically

- The debate takes place within the context of an unequal distribution of power between the sexes

- The patriarchal values and structures of society mean that the activities of women are always seen as less significant than those of men

- An essentialist and somewhat stereotypical view of women as nurturing and men as aggressive needs re-examination, particularly since this may lead to a justification of women and men typically holding certain roles

- Using a female 'lens' to view society is not the norm and that doing so will bring a fresh perspective

- Men are constrained by a particular stereotypical view of masculinity.

The statistics from many countries and work contexts seem to indicate that the inequitable distribution of power between men and women is more than a matter of national or regional cultures and does indicate a more deep-seated and profound discrimination. This provides the context for examination of issues relating to women and men headteachers in England and Wales.

The perspective of the book

This book's perspective is based on the views of the women headteachers, looking back at their experience and reflecting upon it. However, it also examines the views of men headteachers on the same issues. Drawing on both sets of experiences, the main areas that are explored include career paths, combining career and family, stereotypes faced by women and men headteachers and the ways in which the women and men perceive their own management and leadership styles. Consideration is also given to what it feels like to be a woman headteacher and what is special about it. As the book starts from the recognition of the under-representation of women as headteachers, it concludes with an overview of the lessons for women who aspire to headship and the implications for those who lead and manage schools today. Each chapter summarises the points that relate to these two groups. The primary focus is on the position of women in the context of the discrimination and dominant values of society. But I hope that the discussion of headship from the viewpoint of gender will be useful to men as well as women and will allow a fresh insight into striking a balance both in society in general and in the lives of the individuals within it.

2
Building a career as headteacher: the success factors

- How can I make it to the top? What can be learned from the experience of today's heads?

- Who is likely to offer help and support on the way?

This chapter and the following three chapters are all concerned with the patterns of career followed by the headteachers of secondary schools in England and Wales. This chapter takes us through the stages leading up to headship, Chapter Three focuses on acquiring the role and Chapters Four and Five concentrate on a key theme of the book – the mutual influence of career on family and family on career.

Models of career

Individuals typically move through distinct career stages during their working lives: establishment, advancement, maintenance, and withdrawal (Hall, 1976). Similarly, van Eck *et al* (1996) outline a model that distinguishes three chronological phases, anticipation or preparation, then acquisition, and finally performance. Merging these two models together:

- **Preparation** might include obtaining initial qualifications and laying down career plans

- For an aspiring headteacher, **establishment** would be the stage of entering teaching and the lower levels of management

- The **advancement or development** career stage involves gaining new experiences, further qualifications, undertaking special assignments, promotions to more senior levels of management involving the move to other schools and support from others including senior management (Hellriegel, *et al*, 1992)

• **Acquisition** and **performance** relate to obtaining and carrying out the role of headteacher.

This chapter considers the ways in which the women and men who responded to the survey moved through the preparation, establishment and advancement stages of their careers. Chapter Three considers in detail the acquisition of the role of headteacher and later chapters explore aspects of how the women and men perform the role.

The preparation and establishment stages

Most of the headteacher respondents hold a BA or a BSc. Only about five per cent of the men and women heads have a B.Ed (see Table 2.5). At the stage of preparation, the choice of specialist subject area might be important in obtaining headship. However, in their choice of subjects, the differences between the sexes are not great. The most popular specialist areas among the female headteachers are English and humanities. The most popular for the men are humanities and science, representing a slight bias towards the 'hard' curriculum areas that tend to be identified with males (McMullan, 1993).

Table 2.1: Specialist subject of headteachers	women %	men %
English	26.1	16.0
Humanities	21.3	34.8
Science	14.0	20.5
Modern Languages	10.4	6.2
Mathematics	9.0	11.4
Creative	2.0	1.5
Technology	0.9	2.0
Other	16.0	7.7

In their survey of headteachers, Weindling and Earley (1987) found that the biggest difference in subject area between the sexes was that many of the women held English degrees, but in their survey the difference was much greater than appears now. The headteachers in the present survey came from a wide range of specialisms, covering both 'male' and 'female' subjects. The range of specialist subjects is considerable, particularly for the women, and includes in the 'other' category, classics, physical education, information technology and business studies. It may be that the subject range from which headteachers are now drawn is less restricted than in previous years. It also appears that women are slightly less likely to have come from a 'traditional' subject background than the men.

There are potential links between areas of subject expertise and issues of career progression. For example, it is possible that being head of department in certain subject areas may be regarded as good training for more senior posts. The most popular specialisms of all the headteachers were in subject areas where there would typically be a number of staff to 'manage', as opposed to having experience in a single person department in a subject area like music or economics.

Other factors likely to be important in the preparation stage of career are the extent to which an individual actually makes plans for the future and also the range of influences that affect how they make their plans

Career planning

The women and men of the surveys reported in this book were mature and had established themselves in senior positions, which would seem to indicate a degree of determination. However, one of the most notable things about the career progress of a proportion of both sexes, but particularly women, was the 'unexpected' nature of their achievement in becoming heads.

Table 2.2: When did they formulate a career plan that included being a headteacher?

	women %	men %
At school	3.1	4.3
In higher education	1.6	4.0
On becoming a teacher	10.2	20.3
On gaining a post of responsibility	46.1	47.5
Never	21.7	14.5
Other	17.3	9.5

There was a difference between the sexes in planning. A larger proportion of men had taken a decision to become a head relatively early in their career, for example while a teacher. But this group still only represents a minority of the men. Most of them, like the women, were more likely to identify what they wanted only when they had a post of responsibility and were therefore in the establishment stage of their career. Those who did not formulate a plan early in their career tended to be the ones who had harboured doubts about achieving headship.

The larger numbers of women who 'never' identified a career path and the uncertainty about career planning indicated by those who stated 'other' meet Gold's (1996) suggestion that women may just 'drift' into headship. Those women who claimed to have never formulated a career plan were more likely to be in the older age group and were also slightly more likely to be heads of all-girls' schools, with 26.9 per cent claiming that they had never formulated a career plan. Perhaps it is possible that career progress in girls' schools is slightly more 'automatic' than in other schools, and may require less planning ahead. Possibly the presence of children may even encourage ambitious mothers to think ahead, as only 15.9 per cent of the women with children said they had never formulated a career plan. Responses from the female heads illustrate the sometimes piecemeal nature of women's career planning:

> I have applied for interesting jobs as they have arisen – no single path mapped out.

> I didn't [plan] – opportunities presented themselves.

or even:

> What plan?

Although fewer in number, the men who claimed not to have formulated a clear career plan gave evidence of a more 'laid-back' approach and testified to the existence of a number of 'mavericks' amongst the heads:

> I'm uncomfortable linking the words 'career' and 'plan'. A commitment to education and a low boredom threshold have probably been the key factors.

Although one appeared to triumph from adversity, claiming that he decided to become a head:

> After leaving school – branded a failure – [I] received encouragement to develop my skills as a judo instructor.

Many of the surveyed headteachers, both male and female, said that they had not considered headship until they were established as a deputy, emphasising the need to 'plan one step at a time':

> I only decided to be a deputy headteacher as Head of Faculty (female head)

> As my work developed, I assessed each stage. (female head)

> In a very vague way – I haven't really had a coherent plan – it's been more a case of looking at the next step and not much beyond. (male head)

Despite this similarity there are significant differences between the men and the women. Possibly the most important difference relates to the 20 per cent of men who decided on their career aspiration at the point of being a teacher, as opposed to the ten per cent of the women who did so at that time. There are examples of the traditional 'male' form of planning in the responses of some of the male heads, but this was not the case among the female heads. One of the male headteachers put down his success to informed career planning:

> I got right down to the nitty gritty of what was important. Maths = early head of department. Do timetables = get deputy headship. Age 30 = get headship.

Another acknowledged looking two steps ahead rather than one: 'i.e. if I go for this post where could I go next?'

Overall, it seems that planning a career during the preparation stage is relatively rare, particularly for women.

Influences on career choice

Some of the earliest family influences may be particularly important for women. All five of the headteachers interviewed (Coleman, 1996a, p.329) shared some similarities in their backgrounds. All came from families where education was highly valued and where expectations of them were high. In several cases they and in some cases their siblings, were the first in their families to go to university.

> I'm one of a family of six and it's six graduates, three male and three female, and my parents were just absolutely determined that we would use our abilities as best we could. (Andrea)

For one, the family had particularly strong expectations for the women:

> Most of the girls are professionals, teachers, one architect, one dentist, one social worker and so on and the boys in the family aren't. I come from a family where women are traditionally professional people. (Barbara)

The interviewed heads resembled the heads in Hall's (1996) study who had been subject to a range of positive influences from their own homes, particularly, in that case, the influence of their father. The survey for this book showed that the biggest single influence on the head-teachers was their spouse/partner. The influence of parents is rated higher by women than by men, whilst the influence of their own teachers is rated as more important by male headteachers (see table 2.3). The women were more likely to name a range of influences, with more of them mentioning headteachers, parents, friends and colleagues. Both the men and women wrote in 'others' who were influential and for the men, these were mostly colleagues or senior staff where they had worked and there were very few mentions of family members. By contrast, the women who wrote in 'others' mentioned a range of people, mainly family members including aunts, sisters and children, and also the religious community. Both men and women mentioned the im-portance of 'self': 'My own ambition'; 'My own motivation'; 'Myself – I got bored'.

Table 2.3: Career path influences on headteachers			
	women %		men %
Husband/partner	46.0	Wife/partner	46.8
A headteacher or deputy	26.4	Headteacher	11.9
Parents	26.0	Parents	16.5
Friends	21.7	Friends	16.0
Colleagues	17.9	Colleagues	16.7
Own teachers	17.9	Own teachers	26.2

There are similarities in the relative importance of the influences, but for women there appears to be a wider range of influences and more of a stress on the importance of partners and families. The greater importance of teachers' influence for the men links with the slightly higher likelihood of men deciding on a career early in their lives.

The advancement or development stage

Once teachers are established, the way they might move through a variety of middle management roles is likely to be crucial to their development towards headship. One of the basic aspects of this stage is the type and number of roles that an individual holds. Stereotyping about gender roles or holding the 'wrong' post may be a factor affecting the ultimate career success of an aspiring headteacher. One of the main influences, which limit career progress, especially of women, may be gender stereotypes about certain jobs. Davies and Gunawardena (1992) identified the clear differentiation of roles in schools on a gender basis across a range of countries. The kinds of roles associated with men, for example curriculum related, are likely to make men more visible and identify them with management and leadership positions. Roles generally associated with women are the caring and pastoral roles, which are less visible.

Such stereotypes can act negatively on both men and women. For example, they may dissuade men from becoming nursery or primary school teachers, and they also define the perceptions of what a woman is capable of achieving. Probably the most common stereotype about women relates to some of the essentialist ingrained values of society that equate women with caring roles in the family and presume that they will naturally take on the equivalent role in a work situation. Such pastoral roles can be very demanding but rather diffuse, giving experience that is specific to the school and which may then be considered not transferable and less important than the 'harder'and more straightforward roles (Weightman, 1989). These diverse caring roles do not provide good experience for promotion, as this is more likely to follow purely academic or curricular experience (Weindling and Earley, 1987). Even where the role is not necessarily defined as pastoral, women are more likely to be expected to take on a caring or servicing role, for example looking after a child who is ill, or taking the notes at a meeting.

Although one of the problems for women may be their identification with pastoral roles, posts of pastoral responsibility were almost equally common in the life histories of the male and female heads in the surveys. This may indicate a reduction in stereotyping for women or suggest that the women who are determined enough to become heads consciously avoid taking on pastoral roles.

The large proportion who indicated that they had held the post of head of department combined with the overwhelming proportion who had been deputy head, appears to indicate that for most of the headteachers, there had been a rather traditional career progression – a first stepping-stone to departmental head, a more senior post, and finally deputy head-ship, leading to headship (see Table 2.4).

Table 2.4 Posts previously held

	women %	men %
Head of Department	73.0	83.0
Post of Pastoral responsibility (e.g. head of house)	41.9	43.4
Senior teacher or equivalent	32.6	45.4
Head of Faculty	18.9	32.3
Other	24.0	13.3

It was more common for men to have held the post of head of depart-ment plus the relatively senior post of head of faculty or senior teacher or equivalent. It seems that men have tended to hold more jobs of a senior type than women on their progress to headship. The evidence from Weindling and Earley (1987) was that men stayed in posts for shorter periods than women and thus might experience a greater diver-sity of roles.

Other posts, particularly for the women, show diversity. The most popular posts were advisory teachers and advisers for the Local Educa-tion Authority (LEA). Others included: responsibility for the sixth form; Technical and Vocational Education Initiative (TVEI) responsi-bility; head of careers; examinations officer; librarian; school coun-sellor; staff development co-ordinator; special educational needs co-ordinator; industry links co-ordinator and in two cases, lecturing in higher education.

Overall, most of the heads had followed a career path that led through a progression of middle management roles (more of these for men) to deputy headship and headship. Evetts (1994, p.6) notes that the twenty headteachers she studied had similar career progress, being promoted via the curricular route as heads of subject departments.

Development opportunities and gatekeepers

The most crucial stage of career progress is the advancement or development phase in schools (Hill and Ragland, 1995; Gupton and Appelt Slick, 1996). It may be at this phase of working life that women are less favoured, missing out on opportunities such as attending conferences, or representing a group within the school. Van Eck *et al* (1996) consider that men who are in the position to allocate such opportunities often unwittingly give significant opportunities to young men, rather than women. In this analysis they may be drawing on the work of Schmuck (1986) who had emphasised the potential importance of male 'gatekeepers'. Still (1995) refers not only to the glass ceiling but also to the 'glass walls' of stereotyping and 'sticky floors' which may prevent women leaving the more junior ranks of management. Ruijs (1993) comments on the informal male networks and resulting development opportunities that are likely to benefit young male teachers in school:

> Where women have limited access to this type of informal system, they are then less likely to have informal training opportunities such as committee work, quasi-administrative duties and temporary management assignments. [...] This puts female applicants at a disadvantage when competing for management positions against men who have had such opportunities. (p.574)

There was a general awareness on the part of the female headteachers in the survey of the power of gatekeepers. Some women referred to difficulties where there was the absence of a female gatekeeper or the presence of a strong-minded obstructive male who might bar the path:

> On three occasions I was short-listed for headship and was told in private that I was the best candidate, but the mainly male panel couldn't bring themselves to appoint a woman.

Alternatively they could be held back where there were no female role models:

> My first attempts to get a headship were in an LEA where there were no women heads at secondary schools.

In addition, the most important gatekeepers of all, the interview panel for selection of headteachers, tended to be predominantly male. The average numbers of men and women on the panel reported by the headteachers were seven men, and less than three women.

During this period of advancement, women and men who aspire to headship are likely to try to obtain further qualifications.

Table 2.5: Highest qualifications of female and male headteachers		
Qualification	women	men
	%	%
Cert. Ed.	6.4	5.8
B. Ed.	5.8	4.4
BA/B.Sc.	43.8	30.1
Masters	42.0	52.4
Doctorate	1.1	2.7
Other	0.9	3.9

Overall, there are similarities in the qualifications held by men and women but the most significant difference is that a master's degree is held by over 50 per cent of the men, ten per cent more than the women. A similar difference applied in the findings of Weindling and Earley (1987), although at that time only 35 per cent of the male and 21 per cent of the females held a higher degree. In the USA, Shakeshaft (1989) reported that 71 per cent of male secondary school principals held graduate degrees compared with under half of the women. Figures in the UK show the increased popularity, or possibly the growing necessity, of holding a master's degree. Both men and women under 50 are more likely to hold a master's degree than their older colleagues. For women, the difference between the age groups is statistically significant. Having children does not appear to reduce the likelihood of a woman holding a masters degree, since 44.2 per cent of those with children have master's degrees, against an average of 42 per cent.

The findings of Gold (1993), and the relatively large numbers of women candidates for National Professional Qualification for Headteachers (NPQH) point towards a trend for women to equal or even outnumber men on many educational management courses. This has also been observed in the USA, even though men may still dominate the content and teaching of these courses (Worrall, 1995).

Applications for NPQH training show that the numbers of women accepted exceed the numbers of men, but there is still an overall imbalance when the proportion of teachers who are women are taken into account (Whitehead, 1997).

A final stage in the development phase of career is obtaining a deputy headship and there is certainly strong anecdotal evidence of gender stereotyping at this stage for women. However, gender also impacts on the success of men in achieving deputy headship, or at least their perceptions of success.

Obtaining a deputy post: last stage on the route to headship
The vast majority of the headteachers (97 per cent of both men and women) had held the post of a deputy headteacher for an average of about five years (5.6 years for men). Approximately ten per cent, but more women than men, had been a deputy twice and the second post had averaged about four years. The difference between the men and women in terms of holding two deputy posts may be partially explained by women wishing to move to co-educational schools. There was a perception of the narrowness of the experience of a girls' school and working in one was seen to be less useful than working in mixed schools:

> I had to move from deputy head of a girls' school to deputy head of a mixed school before I'd be eligible for headship according to LEA advice. (female head)

> Within the structure girls' schools are thought easy to manage even in inner London. (female head)

The role of the female deputy head has been subject to research that indicates that it has tended to be a gender-stereotyped role. In particular, the work of Litawski (1992) on the female deputy head showed that roles emphasising social-emotional and lower status tasks associated with cleanliness were common. The current research with women heads clearly revealed knowledge of the same type of role. References to being in charge of 'notice-boards', 'flowers' and 'coffee' were aspects of at least some female deputy heads' roles:

> Claire, the oldest of those interviewed, when appointed as a deputy, had been given hostile treatment and an archaic job description which stated that she could not speak at meetings or interfere with the curriculum, but that she could look after such things as the flowers, and arranging social matters for the school. (Coleman, 1996a, p.320)

Commenting on appointment and selection, female headteachers in the survey gave examples of the expectations brought about by both male and female stereotypes:

> Expectations that I would be pastoral care – look after the girls/flowers/coffee/tampax machines.

> Interviewed for head of science, the Governors considered it odd that I should want such a male dominated subject.

This stereotyping of women into caring roles can be seen as the negative aspect of the essentialist feminism outlined in Chapter One. The identification of women with particular attributes such as 'caring' links them with the emotional and irrational and implicitly inferior status of such 'female' work. This work also tends to be operational rather than strategic compared with the rational, more esoteric and implicitly superior status of 'male' work in areas like curriculum and finance. The potential stigma that is associated with the sort of work usually undertaken by women was implicitly recognised by one male headteacher, who commented on the 'unusual nature' of his career progression to headship via being a special educational needs co-ordinator (SENCO).

Despite all this, the stereotype of female members of senior staff tending to be found in pastoral posts (Weightman, 1989, Litawski, 1992) is not fully supported by the survey data (see table 2.6). For 53.6 per cent of the women, curriculum was their main responsibility when a deputy, against 37.7 per cent indicating pastoral/discipline. However, responsibility for curriculum was still much more likely to be held by men than women.

Table 2.6: Indication of main responsibility as deputy head

	women %	men %
Curriculum	53.6	76.8
Pastoral/discipline	37.7	14.0
Personnel	11.1	5.8
Premises	5.3	0.5
Other		3.0

The relatively large number of women involved in curriculum as deputies suggests that more women are now aware of the stereotype of the caring female deputy and are consciously avoiding such roles, ensuring that experience before deputy headship equips them for a range of responsibilities. Two of the female heads commented:

> I always felt I had to avoid the 'female deputy' role – so in some ways my pastoral experience was actually quite limited compared with curriculum/ financial.

> Not accepting the traditional role of female deputy – sick children and flowers!

The work of McBurney and Hough (1989) also suggests that female deputy heads are aware of the need to adopt a more diversified role than the old stereotype suggests.

At the level of deputy, there is perception on the part of a small proportion of the men that some schools show a preference for appointing a female deputy. This is linked to the idea that the school wants to ensure that there is a gender balance amongst their senior managers:

> As a prospective deputy I was very aware of schools attempting to boost female representation on their Senior Management Team.

A few of the men reported historical instances of positive discrimination, particularly in London in the 1970s and 1980s, or recognised that women were preferred for girls' schools.

Support and encouragement for promotion

The support of a senior manager, particularly a previous headteacher, was the most likely encouragement for all the headteachers. However, women are more likely than men to have been encouraged by people outside the school, particularly a partner or other family member, in the same way that family influences on career planning were stronger for women. Qualitative research (Hall, 1996; Coleman, 1996a) has identified the value of support from husband or partner rather than any formal network or group. The support of senior managers appears to be relatively more important for the younger men and this seems to tie up with the idea of the gatekeeper and the suggestion that younger men are more likely to be groomed for promotion (Schmuck, 1986).

Table 2.7: Encouragement for promotion by age group				
	women under 50 %	over 50 %	men under 50	over 50
Headteacher	77.6	75.5	74.7	71.3
Partner and family	64.5	64.2	52.7	50.9
Senior Managers	61.2	58.6	70.4	59.2
Other colleagues	45.2	56.1	55.3	44.4
Others	12.2	20.9	8.1	9.3

Amongst the 'others' category, the most common for both men and women were LEA personnel, officers and advisers. The overall influence of previous headteachers is clear. Associated with this influence may be the importance of mentoring as an aspect of career development.

The importance of mentors and role models

Mentoring is generally recognised as useful, if not essential, in inducting someone new to a post. However, longer term mentoring can go beyond induction to include the concepts of 'sponsorship', 'coaching' and 'counselling', which all imply a more positive role, usually for a senior manager in guiding another's career. It is this aspect of mentoring, formal or informal, which may be particularly valuable in advancing the careers of young, able teachers. Mentoring is considered particularly important in the development of female leaders (Evetts, 1990, Hill and Ragland, 1996, Grogan, 1996) who may need support and encouragement additional to that offered to men because of the cultural perception of the leader as male.

The vast majority (over 90 per cent) of the headteachers had been encouraged to aim for promotion, but only about 55 per cent of the women and men actually claimed to have had someone they actively recognised as a mentor and of these about 60 per cent named a previous headteacher. Those interviewed all commented on the helpfulness of a previous head:

> She [the head] encouraged me to go for headship and probably more than any other person in my career, has been a mentor in that respect. She certainly was very instrumental in helping me to think about headship and obviously in preparing me for it. (Coleman, 1996a, pp.323-4)

In a tiny minority of cases men and women identified that they were re-acting against a bad role model:

> I've seen some poor heads and I thought I could do at least as well! (male head)

In some cases it was specified that the headteacher mentor in question had been male or female. Although only two men said that they had been mentored by women, the women had been mentored by men as often as by women. The importance of male mentors for women as well as men is not unusual – there have been, and continue to be – more men in positions of authority than women and they are usually seen as more able to act as career sponsors (Kram, 1983, Hurley and Fagensson-Elan, 1996). Women as mentors do provide appropriate role models but there are fewer of them in positions of power, and, as mentors and career sponsors, they may be seen as being less influential in the organisation than their male equivalents. Mentoring, both formal and informal, appears to be less available to women; for example, informal mentoring in industry and commerce has tended to be identified with men (Davidson and Cooper, 1992).

With headteachers the most common mentors, other potential mentors included deputy heads, inspector/advisers, heads of department and a range of others including family members and friends. The younger men and women were significantly more likely to have had a mentor than their older colleagues, showing the increasing recognition of the importance of mentoring in career development.

Individuals named as mentors or role models were higher education tutors, an industrial/business partner, or well-known figures in the field of education. However, they tended to be same-sex role models: Ted Wragg, Tim Brighouse, Harry Rea and Derek Glover were specifically mentioned by male heads and Anne Jones, Anita Highams, and Margaret Maden by female heads. For the women, there was also mention of the impact of several courses, including a LEA Women into Management course and a course run by the Industrial Society.

Certain whole schools could be identified as having a supportive ethos. One headteacher (Coleman, 1996a) commented that she was:

> ...just surrounded by these incredibly high calibre teachers, and you just couldn't help but learn, so they were all role models for me and if I hadn't have gone to that school I don't think I would be where I am now. (p.323)

The fact that nearly half of the headteachers stated that they had not had a mentor does not necessarily mean that mentors are not valued. One headteacher wrote that:

> I've never had what I would call a role model – indeed I've often felt the lack of someone to learn from. I think I've had to make my own style and learn by my own mistakes. Nor have I been aware of anyone I could think of as a mentor, though since I became a Head I have tried to act in that role for a number of young women, and see that as part of my job.

The idea of the heads themselves acting as role models for other women is considered in Chapter Nine, which looks at the headteachers' attitudes to career development of their staff, particularly their female staff.

Career Patterns of the Headteachers

The headteachers who responded to the survey had all made it. It is therefore not surprising that many had followed what might be termed a 'male' model that involves a steady career progression, whether planned or unplanned, up a ladder of promotion (Goffee and Nicholson, 1994). However, the women show a tendency to be slightly more diverse in their experience, certainly in terms of the range of subjects from which they are drawn and also at the level of their middle management roles, where they were more likely to have had experience outside school, for example in the local authority or in higher education.

At this stage, the career patterns of the headteachers are being considered without fully taking into account the impact of marriage and children. It is difficult and rather artificial to do this, but in Chapter Four the differential effects of family on women's and men's careers are considered.

The pattern followed by the typical headteacher, whether male or female, appears to have followed a steady progression:

Preparation and anticipation phase

- Only a tiny minority planned their career.

- More women than men were influenced in their career plan by their families.

- More men than women were influenced in their career plan by their teachers.

- Initial qualification was typically a first degree – a BA or BSc rather than a B Ed for both men and women.

Establishment phase

- Subject teaching, most typically English or humanities for women and humanities or science for men. Women show more variety in their subject backgrounds.

- Twice as many men as women decide at this point that they want to become heads.

Advancement or development phase

- Typically, men and women hold the post of head of department, but men are more likely to have also held another senior post in school, women to have had more diverse experience.

- 'Gate-keepers' may inadvertently (or even consciously) favour men.

- A large proportion of men and women decide to become heads at this point.

- Headteachers and colleagues give encouragement to all; family encouragement is more important to women.

- Mentoring is important to both men and women. The relative absence of senior female figures means that women are as likely to be mentored by men as women.

- More men than women gain a master's degree and a doctorate on the route to headship.

- Deputy headship – more women than men are likely to have held two deputy posts. Most common responsibility as deputy is for curriculum, particularly for men, whilst women are still more than twice as likely as men to have had responsibility for pastoral matters or for personnel.

Acquisition – Headship

- A minority have still not planned to become heads and more of these are women!

Confidence and career planning

Possibly one of the most surprising findings is the number of heads who have simply 'drifted' into headship. This lack of planning is linked in some cases to a lack of confidence in their own ability. Lack of confidence was evident amongst both sexes.

> I didn't know that I wanted it or was capable! (female head)

> While a deputy in a closing school, I had to move up faster than I would have wished. It took me a long time to make the psychological leap that I was a head-in-waiting. (female head)

> When I was in my first two posts I never imagined I had the ability. (male head)

Issues relating confidence to career planning, particularly for women, are evident in research in both the USA and the UK. The indications are that women are more likely to expect to have the majority of qualities required for a job whereas men are confident about applying with only some of the qualifications and experience required (Shakeshaft, 1993). Rogers, (1993), commenting on her research in Wales, stated that:

> If a man thought he could perform only three out of the ten duties specified in a job he would still apply for it, whereas if a woman thought she could perform seven out of the ten duties but not the other three she would not apply. (*Education*, 1993, p.151)

For the eight headteachers interviewed by Hustler *et al* (1995):

> The pattern which emerges from the eight interviews is that the men tended to be confident from the outset of their careers – or at any rate early on in them – that headship was their goal, whereas the women had no such expectations. (Rowan, 1995, p.177)

For some of the female heads in the survey, the speed of promotion took the candidate by surprise. Several of the female heads commented on achieving headship at the first try:

> I attempted the first headship interview to gain experience and was appointed!

> I really never had any intention of applying for one – this was my first and only application.

The career success of the headteachers means that they are not typical of the majority of women in education, who do not become senior managers. The interviewed headteachers were actually fairly confident about making applications, and appeared to be making realistic judgements about their own abilities. One of them commented that it would not be necessary to have all the qualities listed in a job description:

> Because I do think there are lost of experiences you have that give you transferable skills, and if you are alert and aware and sensitive, I really do think you can do a lot of very good 'learning on the job'. (Coleman, 1996a, p.324)

Another observed that:

> One of the reasons for moving is to do something that you have not done before. (Coleman, 1996a, p.324)

In having this self-confidence they resembled the headteachers in Hall's research (1996), who made a reasoned assessment of their ability to be heads:

> The women heads demonstrated the possibility of an inner path to headship based on self-efficacy and self-actualisation, a path that is chosen rather than a response to a demand. (p.62)

A lack of confidence linked to feelings of rejection

Experience of rejection often came after many unsuccessful applications and interviews and was actually mentioned more often by men than by women. It was an important factor for the men and perhaps could be linked to the fact that men might have applied for jobs for which they had less experience and qualifications than women which may mean that they are turned down more often. The sometimes devastating effects of rejection were mentioned by women as well as men who, as a result of the rejections, had doubted that they would ever become heads. One man referred to these feelings after doing more than 50 applications for deputy headship, and having ten interviews.

Level of confidence linked to being a woman

Significantly, it was the women who specifically mentioned doubts associated with their gender. They related their lack of confidence to the fact that they were women in an environment where leaders are expected to be male, or compared themselves unfavourably to men:

> after four interviews, some self doubt, as all successes were male.

Others were simply aware that men were more likely to become heads and doubted whether they would ever receive headships. One mentioned:

> six unsuccessful interviews ... all except one were given to a man.

> after about the sixth interview when I was being turned down by some awful schools. I couldn't believe I'd get a decent one – which I did. (female head)

In some cases female candidates were struggling against a male 'agenda':

> ... I failed to be appointed head having done a great job as acting head for eighteen months. The chairman of governors constantly used the phrase 'when the new headmaster comes'.

> After about the fourth headship interview, the sense that governing bodies seemed overwhelmingly conservative, opting for the safe candidate (i.e., usually middle-aged, male, second headship).

Level of confidence – male issues

The men did not make comments relating to gender, except in relation to the 'balance' of the senior management team but there were comments about their individuality from those who felt they did not fit the mould of the (male) stereotype of headteacher. These few men seemed to have rejected the dominant brand of masculinity (Collinson and Hearn, 1996) and therefore have something in common with the women for whose gender made them 'outsiders' (Schmuck, 1996). In one case a head thought his politics would be against him; another commented that: 'As a deputy, I missed a number of posts at interview: I appear (and am) odd.' Others hinted at being blocked, one that he was: '...too challenging, not a typical grey suit type.' Being an individual or being idiosyncratic in some way may be particularly unacceptable at a time when it is thought that there is a move towards managerialism: 'rational, data-driven systems' (Lumby and Tomlinson, 2000, p.140), a concept that has much in common with the standard male stereotype of leader.

Confidence, career planning and personal circumstances

A large minority of the surveyed heads, both men (44 per cent) and women (43 per cent), indicated that they had harboured doubts about their ability to obtain headship. Amongst the women, those who were most likely to have doubts were those now over 50, who were married and had children. The impact of domestic decisions, difficulties and responsibilities seems to play a large part in nurturing doubts about career progress.

Although the younger men were less likely than older men to have experienced doubt, there was not as great a difference as between the two age groups of the women. It seems that some of the younger child-less women are more determined and have been less likely to doubt their progress than any other group. This may be linked to a conscious decision to not have children (see Chapter Four) and a conscious avoidance of the problems that might be linked to gender such as differential development opportunities.

For both men and women there were reports of particular family circumstances or circumstances related to their region that affected their planning. These included a small number of male and female heads who had been ill and two of the male heads whose wives had died and who had to take family responsibility. One male and one female head commented on the use of the Welsh language as being an issue that is important for appointment in Wales and one female head observed that: 'I am American' implying all sorts of difficulties. Other comments from male heads related to the disinclination to become a head at the time of union trouble in the 1970s and 1980s, and a few to having considered an alternative career.

Reading the comments from the women and the men reveals similarities in terms of the experience of rejection and lack of planning in particular but marked differences in terms of the negative perceptions of gender experienced by the women, which impacted on their confidence levels.

Conclusion

The route to headship is difficult for both men and women. Both sexes have experience of rejection and may lack confidence about taking on this difficult job. For a surprisingly large proportion, there is a lack of planning and even an element of surprise in finding themselves a head-teacher. What is significantly different is the perception by the women that their gender is 'against them' in becoming a headteacher, something that no man ever considers. They are also likely to encounter stereotyping that is unhelpful in making career progress. Although women appear to be waking up to the difficulties stereotyping might cause them, the fact remains that culturally, certain 'male' jobs are considered more fitting as preparation for headship. In the next chapter, the appointment process to headship is explored in more detail.

Learning points for aspiring women:

- Early planning is not essential for success but note that men are more likely to plan than women

- The first degree subject of choice for headteachers is one of the humanities; being head of this relatively diverse department seems to allow early management opportunities

- Aim for a spread of experience and stay wary of pastoral 'pigeon-holing'

- Look for, and take the small but significant career opportunities e.g. a visible role as a short-term project leader

- Be sure to have a mentor, probably a male one

- Don't be put off by rejection

- Don't feel that you have to have all the qualities listed in the job specification.

Learning points for headteachers:

- Ensure that women are considered for the small but significant career opportunities that you might offer to young middle managers

- Value the experience that middle managers and senior managers gain through pastoral responsibilities

- Offer mentoring widely.

3

Becoming a headteacher

- How can I make it to the top? What can be learned from the experience of today's headteachers?

Continuing the story, this chapter considers the headteachers at the point at which they are reaching the peak of their career. At this stage, what are the factors that differ in the experiences of men and women? What is helpful to them in achieving headship? In particular, what are their experiences of interview and appointment?

The majority of the headteachers surveyed, slightly more of the women (84.2 per cent) than the men (77.9 per cent) were in their first headship. At the time they were asked, the average length of headship for both was seven years.

The time of life when the status of head is achieved is of key significance. The overall age range is similar for men and women. The headteachers are mainly in their forties and fifties with very few under 40 or over 60. (see Table 3.1). It is unusual for a headteacher of either sex to be appointed earlier than age 40, and it is almost equally unusual for them to remain in post once they reach 60. However, there is one major difference: the women are much more likely to be appointed to a headship during their forties.

Table 3.1 : Age groups of headteachers		
	women %	men %
30 – 39	0.9	1.9
40 – 49	53.6	43.2
50 – 59	42.3	51.2
60 and over	1.5	2.2

In a way this is surprising, although the average age of heads as a whole has not changed from what Jones (1987) reported over twenty years ago, with about half of them under and half over 50, there has definitely been a change in the average age of the appointment of female head-teachers. All previous research in the UK and also in the USA has indicated that women headteachers and principals were older than their male colleagues (Gross and Trask, 1976; Weindling and Earley, 1987; Shakeshaft, 1989; Evetts, 1994). Weindling and Earley (1987), working with two groups, one of new and the other of existing 'old' heads, considered the differences in age both between the groups and between the male and female members of each. In both cases the women were older than the men. Evetts (1994) noted that of the twenty headteachers she studied, the ten men were in their late thirties or early forties when appointed, the ten women in their late forties or early fifties. It seems that in relatively recent years there has been a distinct shift in the UK to appoint more women heads who are in their forties, and relatively young in comparison with the men, the majority of whom are in their fifties. The appointment of more women than men in the younger age group does seem a little surprising, given the general understanding that the promotion of women to high status jobs may be delayed by time off for childbirth and childcare.

Without doubt, an important factor in becoming a female head is the existence of a relatively large number of girls' schools.

Table 3.2 Proportion of headteachers in co-ed and single sex schools		
	women headteachers %	men headteachers %
Co-ed schools	66.8	91.3
Girls only schools	32.4	0.5
Boys only schools	0.7	8.2

The evidence from both surveys is that it is generally expected that a woman will head up a girls' school, and that a man will head a boys' school Indeed only two of the men in the survey are heads of girls' schools and only three women are heads of boys' schools, less than one per cent of the respondents in each case. Several comments from the women related to their unsuccessful applications for mixed schools, followed by success when they applied to a girls' schools:

> Then I applied for an all-girls' school, which I had not done previously. This immediately brought me my first interview and I got the job. At my first Secondary Heads' Meeting I realised that I was the only women secondary head in that Borough – there was, after all, only one girls' school! (female head)

However, experience in girls' schools may be seen as inferior and may in turn lead to experience of discrimination in relation to employment:

> I've never got anywhere with applications for co-ed schools but I have always been in girls schools, therefore 'limited' experience! (female head)

Men who worked in boys' schools reported no such experience of being seen as 'limited'.

Although a head of the same sex is favoured for a single sex school, the impact of this is much greater for women than for men. A third of all the women were heads of same sex schools against under ten per cent of the men. It looks as if a reduction in the numbers of girls' schools would be likely to lead to an overall reduction of the numbers of women headteachers.

Obvious differences between men and women heads can also be seen in the matter of is location, as mentioned in Chapter One. The further the school is from London, the less likely it is to have a woman headteacher. In the surveys of headteachers reported here, 20 per cent of the women heads came from London but only 9.2 per cent of the men. In contrast, the proportion of men headteachers coming from metropolitan areas, the shire counties and Wales was, always higher.

Within the different regions of the UK there are striking differences in the proportion of female headteachers (Edwards and Lyons, 1994). The most likely explanation for geography being so closely related to equal opportunity for women lies in the prevalence of stereotypes about male and female leadership. The areas where male conservatism about women leaders is strongest are still the areas where attitudes were moulded by heavy industry or rural conservatism:

> A lot of governors in Yorkshire were miners or ex-miners and to them a man is always the boss and a woman's place is in the home. Mind you, when I came to East Anglia, I found that many of the governors I met are farmers with pretty similar attitudes! (Edwards and Lyons, 1994, p.9)

In contrast, London appears to have governors with more 'sophisticated' attitudes, and who may still be affected by the residue of the Inner London Education Authority's (ILEA) influence with regard to equal opportunities:

> They [the ILEA] created the expectation that women could succeed, they put gender on the map. Their equality policies made an enormous difference psychologically, and that has resulted in a steady progression on women's part. (female deputy director of education of a London Borough, quoted by Edwards and Lyons, 1994, p.8)

A comment from one of the female heads in my survey illustrates some of the difficulties related to location:

> I applied for headships in many home counties, south west, south east, east of England shires. Usually I was the only woman short-listed out of six. Often men wore Rotary or similar badges, – as did the panel! People obviously knew each other. I felt I was a 'token' woman, but that the outcome was often pre-determined.

The selection process

The pattern of selection for headship does vary and will now be partially driven in England and Wales by the list of competences identified through the NPQH. Selectors may make use of assessment centres and are likely to include different types of tests and presentations. However, it is certain that at least one panel interview will be a key part of the process despite the fact that interviews are notoriously suspect as a means of making effective choices. Some of the problems with the interview as a selection test include: the importance of physical attraction; the speed at which interviewers make decisions (generally under four minutes) and the tendency for the interview to be used to justify decisions rather than to guide them (Middlewood, 1997, p.150). These points may especially disadvantage women being interviewed for headship, where the stereotypical view of males as more likely to possess leadership qualities is often matched by a stereotype of females as fitted for lesser roles and, when married, as subservient to their husbands.

The answer to problems with interviews would seem to be to improve the methods used in selection. However, more sophisticated methods of assessment in selection do not automatically eliminate gender bias. Looking at the under-representation of women in general management, Alimo-Metcalfe (1994a) surveyed the range of assessment procedures available in business. These included the interview, the use of psycho-metric tests, cognitive ability tests, personality measurement, using assessment centres and the evaluation of ongoing performance. She concluded, somewhat pessimistically, that:

> As organizations purportedly attempt to increase the 'fairness' and 'objec-tivity' of assessment, they may in fact be increasing the effect of gender bias. Furthermore, as the techniques of assessment become more com-plex, sources of bias are far less obvious and hence less likely to be chal-lenged. (Alimo-Metcalfe, 1994a, p.104)

Experience of interviews and of a mainly male panel (see Chapter Two) is common as the main means of selection of headteachers but does not necessarily worry every woman candidate!

> They started off the interview by saying we apologize for the fact that we're all men here, but that's just a challenge for you. I remember thinking, 'yes, well if I go and get the job, it's going to be a challenge for you as well.' (female headteacher, in Coleman 1996a. p.326)

Selection and Sexism

The major studies on selection of heads (Morgan *et al*, 1983, Weindling and Earley, 1987) were done in the 1980s, when the proportion of women heads was smaller than today and when memories of overt and legal discrimination prior to the legislation of the 1970s would have been fresh. Summarising research undertaken in the first half of the 1980s, it seemed that:

> Promoters are operating from constructions of gender roles defined in narrow, traditional terms which accentuate women's roles as wives and mothers and diminish their roles as teachers. (Grant, 1989, p.45)

Memories pre-dating equal opportunities were still present for the female heads in the survey. Some of their retrospective comments cover a considerable period of time and quote examples of overt discrimina-tion:

> In the 1960/70s I was told I was the best candidate, but they gave the job to a man because he was the breadwinner.

One headteacher recalled that when she was applying for Head of Department posts in 1973, when discrimination on grounds of sex was still legal, a school secretary told her:

There's no point in my sending you the details, dear. I know the Head-
master wouldn't even consider appointing a woman to this post.

More recent research into the selection of ten male and ten female heads
(Evetts, 1991, and 1994) noted some changes in the nature of the
selection process, from that described by Morgan *et al* (1983). However,
this research still concluded that:

> There were important elements of continuity in the headteacher selec-
> tion process. Gender differences in the achievement of headteacher posts
> continued to be very large in spite of the claimed objectives of both LEAs
> and teacher unions in their equal opportunities policies. (Evetts, 1991,
> p.293)

Had things changed by the time of the current research at the end of the
1990s?

Despite legislation and a changing culture, the majority of the female
heads in the survey conducted for this book answered that they had
experienced sexism in the selection process. Altogether, 62.5 per cent of
the women heads indicated that they had experienced sexist attitudes at
the time of appointment, the remainder (37.5 per cent) that they had not.
What differentiated those who reported sexism from those who did not?

> Those who were married and had children were much more likely to
> report sexist attitudes than those who were single.

> The heads of girls' schools were less likely to report sexist attitudes.
> Heads of these schools are expected to be women and female candidates
> are therefore presumably less likely to be subject to sexist comment at
> the time of application.

**Table 3.3: % of women headteachers stating that they had experienced
sexism in applications**

	%		%
over 50	61.5	children	67.4
under 50	64.5	no children	57.1
heads of girls' schools	54.3	married	63.4
		single	56.3
heads of other schools	67.8	separated	76.9
		divorced	63.0

The younger headteachers reported sexism more often than their older colleagues (see table 3.3). Is it possible that the younger headteachers were more sensitized than their older peers to potential sexism in respect of their applications, or is sexism more prevalent now, even if less overt?

The headteachers who said they had experienced sexism when applying for jobs were asked to give examples. Some of these relate to their overall experiences in applying for a range of jobs, including head of department and deputy head, as well as applications for headship. There were altogether 325 examples or comments from the women and 135 from the men. The comments from the men will be considered separately. Although the numbers of men responding to the survey were high, they were less likely than the women to comment on sexism and their comments were generally limited to what they had seen women experience.

Despite the fact that equal opportunities legislation has been in place since the 1970s, there are many examples of sexism reported in the survey at the end of the 1990s that might have warranted legal action. In addition to the Human Rights legislation originating in Europe, in the UK all institutions are subject to the legal requirements of the Sex Discrimination Act (1975), the Race Relations Act (1976) and the Equal Pay Act (1970).

Direct discrimination on grounds of race or sex occurs when someone is treated less favourably than others – not being employed simply on grounds of their gender or ethnicity. Potential examples of this abound in the reports of the female headteachers, where the need for a woman to be better than a man in order to succeed was quite overt in some interviews:

> in interview being told I would have to be better than the male applicants.

> it seemed women had to be outstanding in comparison to men to be appointed to a management post.

Other comments related more to the perception that women were simply not as able as men to lead a school:

> feedback from headship interview by the director for secondary education (who was female) was that 'they wanted a man for the job'.

> I was appointed head of a boys' comprehensive – many doubted the wisdom of my appointment and told me so.

The opinion of one of the interviewed heads was that:

> Some governors, I think are very much prejudiced. Having been given this post, they still feel that perhaps there is a man lurking somewhere who is doing the hard-nosed bit. (Coleman, 1996a. p.325)

The effect of these attitudes is invidious and inevitably affects the confidence of applicants. One head observed:

> I used to look at the other interviewees (mainly males) and assume they would be more eligible than me.

Research in the early 1980s had been critical of the assessment procedures adopted by LEAs. It was suggested that the sometimes arbitrary procedures adopted could cause difficulties for all the candidates for headship, but that they might particularly affect the selection of women. In a situation where the majority of those appointing were male it was felt that:

> The variability of criteria used in judging fitness for headship is likely to be complicated still further by the additional criteria which come into play when the candidate is a women. (Morgan et al. 1983 p.73)

In the research undertaken for this book, governors and others on the interview panel were still judging on these 'additional criteria'. One female head reported:

> Some stupid comments from governors at the 'trial by sherry' part.

Another that:

> I was once asked by governors at interview how a little thing like you would discipline a great big boy, would you say 'hey is it cold up there?'

One female head in responding to the question on experience of sexism at the point of application noted:

> ...being groped by an interviewer during lunch.

The interviewed women heads also expressed concern about the behaviour of some governors. One recalled how in an interview:

> A member of the interviewing panel had noisily, and at length, cleaned out his pipe and then moved onto clipping his fingernails in an apparent attempt to sabotage the interview and ensure that a woman was not appointed. (Coleman, 1996a, pp.319-20)

One of the male headteachers in the survey also commented on what would have amounted to a clear breach of the law if allowed to continue:

> Governors at a previous school wanted to go back on the appointment of a female head of department who discovered she was pregnant two days after appointment (we persuaded them that they were out of order!).

Members of the selection panel also made astonishingly personal comments on the appearance of the women candidates. None of the men responding to the survey reported any such remarks.

> An all male panel interviewed me for my Deputy Headship. Apparently they spent a long time discussing whether they were appointing me on merit rather than my personal appearance/qualities.

> From staff and governors (some) who questioned whether a 'small' woman could run large comprehensive school!

> Going for a deputy post – I was told I was only at this stage in my career because of my long legs and pretty face (I had just touched 40!)

> A quote from the Chair of Governors upon accepting this post – 'LEA was not wholly in favour of appointing a 36 year old blonde to such a post, but we liked the look of you!'

Commenting on the interview procedure for women applying for jobs traditionally held by males, Alimo-Metcalfe states that:

> Type of dress, physical attractiveness and even the wearing of lipstick significantly affect the assessor's decision. (Alimo-Metcalfe, 1994b, p.28)

Indirect discrimination may occur when a non-essential requirement for a job has the effect of excluding one gender or ethnic group. For example, several of the women heads said that they had been eliminated from the candidates for headship because of the importance of rugby or cricket in the school.

The women headteachers quoted the most overt examples of direct discrimination from the period before the equal opportunities legislation was in force. However, in the more recent reports there are many examples of what could still be interpreted as either direct or indirect discrimination. The largest single group of comments were related to the presumption that the headteacher would have the major responsibility for childcare and that her husband's job would take precedence and so consequently she would be less likely than a man to do the job well:

> Governing body members suggested the job was too much for someone with children in the headship interview. (female head)

> In my first successful interview, I was asked, whether as a young woman, I intended to start a family. I recall that I felt this was not relevant.

Several of the heads were asked questions along the lines of:

> What does your husband think of this headship lark?

Another head commented on her experience of interviews for secondary headships:

> Where it (sexism) became apparent – everything from subtle questioning re domestic arrangements to one interviewer indicating that my husband must find me intimidating!

There were also several comments relating to the presumption that a husband's job would come first:

> I was asked on applying for my first headship if I would stay in post long as my husband worked further afield.

In addition, there are instances of how discriminatory behaviour is simply taken for granted as part of the unquestioned values of society. There was, for example, the absolute assumption on the part of some schools that the new headteacher would be a man:

> I am still receiving post addressed 'headmaster'.

> When I was interviewed for the present post there was a letter on the headteacher's wall to all governors, inviting them to discuss the appointment of the new headmaster.

Some recognised the existence of sexism and discrimination generally, but felt that they had not actually experienced it themselves:

> Not applied to me personally, but a general atmosphere that some jobs (including headship) are for men. (female head)

> Not so much personally as observing other peoples' experiences and standards for various jobs. (female head)

> Unsure – cannot recall any but feel there have been. (male head)

> Appointing groups favouring one sex over the other. (male head)

Some of the comments from female heads were quite tentative, and illustrate the subtlety of the situation:

> ... but perhaps a little when first applying for headship
>
> ... difficult to decisively prove.

From one member of an interviewing panel, there was an indication of firmly held stereotypes being used in an even-handed way:

> One interviewer asked male candidates if they read educational journals and female candidates if they could ride a bike! (male head)

The women who were answering the question about sexism had been successful, and a few comments indicated this:

> some [sexist] attitudes at interviews, but not a problem.

When studying the attitudes of women administrators in the USA Matthews (1995) has identified four types ranging from those who actively support women to those who deny that there is any problem. One of these groups, the 'isolates' may acknowledge that some women experience discrimination but deny any personal knowledge of it. They are 'detached from issues of equity in administration' (Matthews, 1995, p.256). Research carried out with nineteen female principals in the USA noted that:

> All women reported their femaleness made a difference in their jobs, yet only two principals noted behaviours which they labelled 'discriminatory', although several women reported examples of differential treatment such as, 'they have been less than accepting of me because I am a woman.' How can we make sense out of the fact that they received differential treatment, yet deny the fact of personal discrimination? (Schmuck and Schubert, 1995, p.282)

Some of the headteachers interviewed by the author (Coleman, 1996a, 1996b) initially denied that they had experienced any discrimination but when probed could all recall examples of instances of sexism they had experienced but had given little thought to. The attitude of the heads tended to be pragmatic. When faced with discrimination they would generally choose to 'find a way round it to do what you want to do' (Coleman, 1996a, p.320).

Male experience of sexism

Only a third of the men responded positively in identifying sexist behaviour at the time of appointment. Of these, the majority had in mind sexism experienced by women and witnessed by them as men. Only 55 of 135 comments identified sexism as a barrier to men and most of these comments related to positive discrimination for women and therefore implicitly to barriers for men. Comments about positive discrimination for women referred either to obtaining deputy head gender balance or to the preference, already noted for appointing women to single sex schools.

Most of the other comments of the male headteachers endorsed the comments made by the women about anti-female discrimination, some referring to the importance of boys' sport – a recurring theme with both men and women and a clear example of indirect discrimination:

> The sportsmen have a real advantage! (male head)

> [Twice I have been told that] only men can maintain discipline. In one case, that women cannot project authority even in assembly, and in another that a woman couldn't be trusted to maintain a good rugby team. (female head)

Others simply referred to the general atmosphere of certain schools:

> Some schools have male dominated management and determination to maintain this.

There was also the rare comment that related to the concept of the dominant type of masculinity, termed 'hegemonic' by Collinson and Hearn (2000), raising the question of gender discrimination against males as well as females:

> People make assumptions about male behaviour and about how males will operate. Men who are unconventional face prejudice. (male head)

However, this was an isolated example of one man expressing discomfort because of stereotypes related to male gender.

Conclusion

The research of the 1980s did indicate that for those women who do get as far as applying for headship the chances of achieving success are proportionately as good as a male candidate's. Women only accounted for 11 per cent of the applications for headships of mixed comprehensive schools in 1980-83 and they were also 11 per cent of those appointed (Morgan *et al*, 1983, p.68). The experience of the interviewed heads endorsed this, in that they were successful after a small number of applications and they had generally found the interview procedures to be fair (Coleman, 1996a). In my survey, more men than women also identified rejection following multiple applications for headship.

However, previous research on selection seems to indicate that selectors, who tend to be male, have difficulty overcoming the stereotype of women as linked with the home and family (Morgan *et al*, 1983). More recent research still confirms that this is the case (Grant, 1989; Evetts, 1991, 1994). Only in the research undertaken by Hall (1996) is there an indication of a more open and egalitarian attitude on the part of selection panels. Two of the three secondary heads were surprised at getting the job:

> ... not because they did not consider themselves ready, but because they thought they did not fit the desired stereotype. (p.59)

Despite some indications of change in practice, the survey of men and women headteachers at the end of the twentieth century clearly shows that a majority of women and a proportion of men judge that gender stereotypes, almost exclusively relating to women, still play an important part in the selection of the headteachers for our secondary schools.

Table 3.4 Typology of discrimination experienced by women headteachers

Type	Example
overt discrimination	'the headmaster wouldn't even consider appointing a woman to this post'
direct discrimination	'told I would have to be better than the male applicants.'
sexual harassment	'groped by an interviewer over lunch' comment on 'my long legs and pretty face'
indirect discrimination	'the sportsmen have the real advantage' 'governors wanted to go back on the appointment of a female head when she discovered she was pregnant.'
prevailing social values	'I am still receiving post addressed 'headmaster''. 'not applied to me personally, but a general atmosphere that some jobs including headship are for men.'

Table 3.5 Typology of male experience of discrimination

awareness of discrimination against women	'some schools with male dominated management and a determination to maintain this.'
positive discrimination for women (SMT balance and women heads for girls' school preferred)	'some posts where it became clear that a female appointee was required'.
discrimination against men who do not conform	'Men who are unconventional face prejudice'.

Learning points for aspiring women:

- Don't feel that you are too young to apply

- Consider location: London and the metropolitan areas are statistically favourable

- Women are favoured for girls' schools but these schools can be seen as not offering the full experience of headship

- Be prepared for discriminatory behaviour

- Don't let your confidence be rocked!

Learning points for headteachers:

- Be aware of the extent of hidden prejudice

- Ensure that all concerned with the selection process, including governors, have equal opportunities training.

4
Career and family:
Can there be a balance?

• Will I be able to manage being a parent and having a career?

One of the biggest challenges women and men face today is combining a career that is satisfying with the demands and rewards of family life. The expectation is that both men and women will generally be economically active. The assumption that the male is the main or only breadwinner has all but disappeared, even though stereotypes about male and female roles remain. Women's participation in the work force is expected to continue to increase, although, according to Ruijs (1993, p.545), there is a clear and established relationship between the level of women's employment within European countries and the availability of childcare they provide. Nevertheless, women now comprise over half the British labour force although they account for only three per cent of company directors (Charlesworth, 1997).

Demographic changes affect lives. Although the birth-rate is falling, working adults are responsible not only for childcare but for an element of the care of older people, whose numbers are increasing. There is also some evidence of a re-assessment of the role of men in family life and this is considered more fully in Chapter Five. Changes in expectations about paid work outside the home and the nature and size of the family are immense.

> Increasingly, then, the workforce is composed of women and men with responsibilities for both the care and economic support of families, who seek a balance between their work and private lives. (Lewis, 1996, p.2)

The first key finding from a UK government baseline study on work life balance is that:

There is a high level of support for work-life balance. Many employers agreed that people work best when they can strike a better balance between work and the rest of their lives and that everyone should be able to balance their work and home lives in the way they want. (DfEE, 2000b, p.iv)

Against this level of agreement, findings from the same study showed that about 11 per cent of full-time employees worked 60 or more hours a week, typically those in professional jobs, and that those most likely to work long hours were men in couple households with dependent children. The impact of such long hours on family life and on the partner who does not work such long hours is considerable.

A large proportion of the headteachers in the survey probably worked this long and hard. When asked why they had been successful, 85 per cent of the women and 81 per cent of the men said it was hard work. One of the women headteachers interviewed said about her success: 'I am prepared to work incredibly hard. I have put in a 70 hour week for 15 years' (Coleman, 1996a, p.327).

Given the sort of demands made on such professionals, and the fact that women are still more likely to take the responsibility for children, it is not surprising that many of the women headteachers are not married and that of those who are, many appear to be choosing not to have children.

The most striking difference between the men and women headteachers is not the way they have managed their careers, nor the way that they run their schools, but the impact their career appears to have had on their family life, particularly the decision whether to have children. The proportion of male headteachers who are married is 95 per cent and the proportion of married female headteachers is 67 per cent. In a survey of

Table 4.1 Marital status of female headteachers under and over 50

	under 50	over 50
Married	70.6	64.1
Single	18.5	19.9
Separated	3.2	2.9
Divorced	7.7	13.1

managers carried out for the Institute of Management (Charlesworth, 1997) 80 per cent of the men were married compared to 69 per cent of the women. Like the women headteachers, more of the women managers were likely to be divorced or separated.

Although more of the younger female headteachers are married, the difference between them and their older female colleagues lies more in the proportion that are divorced than in the proportion who remained single. There are considerably more broken marriages amongst the women than the men. For women, ten per cent overall are divorced and 3.1 per cent separated as against 1.5 and one per cent for men. This difference seems to indicate a greater strain on marriage for women headteachers than for men headteachers. This strain may be greatest in dual career families:

> Exposure to stress at work can create tension within marriage, due to negative moods and preoccupation at home, so it can be argued that the potential for tension is greater when there are two stressful jobs. (Lewis, 1994 p.234)

Whether single, divorced or separated, a third of women headteachers live alone in comparison to the five per cent of the men who do so. In the UK as a whole, the figures for all managers are similar to those for the headteachers: 58 per cent of the women are married, but 93 per cent of the men. (Davidson and Cooper, 1992). Although there are some members of religious orders amongst the headteachers, only twenty of the women were likely to have been unmarried because of a vow of celibacy.

When it comes to having children the distinction between the men and the women is even starker. Over 94 per cent of the male headteachers have a child or children compared to only 51.7 per cent of the women. The fact that nearly half the women are childless contrasts with a figure of about 20 per cent for the female population overall (ONS, 2001). Throughout Europe, women managers are much more likely to be single and/or childless than male managers (Vinnicombe and Colwell, 1995).

A number of the female headteachers who had children were single parents. Amongst the female headteachers with children, 17.6 per cent were divorced, separated or widowed. The high marriage rate amongst the men means that very few of them were operating as single parents, although there are a small number (four identified themselves) who took major responsibility for the family due to family circumstances, for example illness or death of his wife. It is notable that these four men responded to many of the questions in the survey in a similar way to many of the women and quite unlike the rest of the men.

Table 4.2 The percentages of male and female headteachers having children		
	All men %	**All women %**
Having a child or children	94.0	51.7
Number of children		
0	5.8	48.3
1	8.2	17.0
2	51.4	27.0
3	25.9	6.6
4	6.8	0.6
5	1.6	0.4
6	0.5	0.0
7	0.5	0.0

The proportion of women under 50 who have children is much lower (statistically significantly so) than for the women over 50, but the numbers of men having children hardly differs between the two age groups.

Women 50 or over with a child or children   61.6 %

Women up to 50 with a child or children   44.4%

In addition, a higher proportion of the over 50s than the under 50s had two or three children. In both age groups and genders four or more children were exceptional, but large families were slightly more common amongst the men.

It appears that many of the younger women are choosing not to have children, in spite of an apparently more egalitarian society which offers maternity leave and guarantees job security for women taking a statutory break. Although maternity leave ensures that a job remains open, it does not help the women who return to work with handling the demands of a baby plus paid work.

It is just possible that a number of those under 50 have not yet completed their families, but the dearth of women headteachers with young children would make that seem unlikely. At the time of the survey only ten of the 470 women respondents had a child under five. Nevertheless the smaller proportion of the younger female headteachers having children compared to those who are slightly older is surprising in view of the face that marriage is at least as popular with the younger women and they had the opportunity of taking statutory maternity leave. The tendency for the younger women to limit their families to one child or to have no children may be a realistic recognition of the continued difficulties associated with career ambition and motherhood. Research with 48 British women identified as 'successful' appeared to show differences between the younger group and the one with an average age of 56:

> It was proposed that the sample consisted of two cohorts who were exposed to different socialization experiences. (White, 2000, p.167)

Women managers in general are less likely to have children than the average woman, and more likely to delay motherhood until their thirties, and may then have only one child (Davidson and Cooper, 1992, Ouston, 1993).

> Combining work with child-rearing continues to be stressful for most women and it is clear that some organisations have compounded this problem by operating a double standard for marriage: they view the married male manager as an asset, with a stable support network at home allowing him to give his undivided attention to his work, but the married female manager as a liability, likely to neglect her career at the expense of her family at every possible opportunity. (Vinnicombe and Colwell, 1995, p.7)

The situation for women headteachers certainly seems to be inimical to achieving a balance between work and family since so many of them, particularly the younger ones, seem to have effectively opted out of trying to combine the two.

What about the men headteachers?

None of the respondents to the survey specifically addressed their decision to have children or not and whether or not to get married. It is the actions of the respondents that speak for them. However, some men made comment that reflect on the burden of their work, revealing that it did impinge on the family and their relationship with their children:

Within my marriage arrangement the 'man' has the public career. I could not do what I do without my wife. In a real sense it takes two people (seven if you include my children) to do my job. All of us have made great sacrifices. Time will tell whether we have been wise. PS. Not one of my children has the slightest interest in being a teacher. (male headteacher)

The conceptualisation of work/life balance

In addressing the issue of work life balance, there are a number of different implicit approaches. Lewis (1996) identifies three basic types.

- Equal opportunities, which in turn can be sub-divided into

  equal access for men and women to paid work

  equal representation for women and men at all levels including management and, more comprehensively, 'to enhance oppor-tunities for men and women to adapt work for family reasons with the diverse work patterns that emerge from these adjust-ments being as equally valued as traditional patterns of work.' (p.8)

- The quality of life argument – finding a balance and reducing the potential for role stress, role conflict and overload en-gendered by the competing elements of work and family.

- The business case, which stresses the advantages to employers of having workers who will give of their best, with reduced levels of stress. This case also incorporates the advantages of maintaining mothers and other carers as economically active.

Chapter One outlined feminist analyses of the situation of women in posts of responsibility in education including the diametrical opposition of the equal opportunities approach (where the status quo is not basically changed) to the critical approaches that seek to change the political and economic structures of society. However, an aspect of the equal opportunities approach that is put forward by Lewis (1996) above, implies not just the maintenance of the status quo but, also the ques-tioning of 'traditional patterns of work' and envisages a society where work patterns may be 'diverse' but are 'equally valued'. Such equal valuing will necessitate the development of a new way of looking at work and family; one which does not automatically endorse the male way of working with its long hours and exclusion of family. In other words, a fairly radical change in society, its values and power structure and one which would affect schools as organisations where adults and young people work. One example offered is the introduction of family leave and the acceptance of more flexible ways of working.

However, the preoccupation with quality of life, role conflict and stress seems to have more resonance with the experience of headteachers, particularly the women, than with any immediate possibility of a re-structured society. The business case may seem logical, but in practice there is little (although slowly growing) recognition by employers of the needs of families.

Childcare and care of other dependants

The majority of the headteachers surveyed had children who were now past the age when childcare is a big issue. Nevertheless for half of the female headteachers, that is those with children, and for 94 per cent of the men, consideration has been given or is still being given to childcare arrangements during the day and before and after school. A clear division emerges. Whereas many of the men named their wife as principal carer, many of the women would have had the experience of taking all or partial responsibility for one or more children at a time when they were likely to have been teaching or progressing up the career ladder beyond classroom teaching.

The headteachers were asked about their main method of childcare provision when their children were young (see Table 4.3). Of the headteachers who were mothers, most had used child-minders. In contrast, most of the men had relied on their wives. Some of the respondents had used more than one type of childcare.

Table 4.3: Nature of childcare adopted by the headteachers

	women %	men %
Child-minder	49.7	27.2
Nursery	27.1	8.3
Relative	23.0 (includes husband)	81.9 (includes wife)
Husband/wife	3.8	70.9
Nanny	20.5	2.9

Most considered the arrangements satisfactory, including over 95 per cent of the female headteachers. Presumably, where there had been problems with childcare, the headteacher concerned had taken steps to put matters right. Slightly more of the men had concerns about the childcare arrangements, although 86 per cent considered them satisfactory. Those who felt it was not mostly spoke about the detrimental effect on the career of their wives because they had responsibility for the childcare. 'But my wife paid high price in terms of her own teaching career' (male head) was a typical comment.

Although wives were the likely carers for the children, not all difficulties in combining work and family were avoided. One male headteacher referred to them managing:

> With flexible working by my wife: I looked after the children at weekends and she worked nights at weekends. She's a nurse.

However, the natural expectation that it will be the woman who takes the lead role in family and childcare imposes a burden on the women heads with children. It was clear that many of the women headteachers were pre-occupied with the guilt engendered by their role conflict as mothers and career women:

> I suffered – not the children.

> I was a pioneer working mother – got lots of disapproval, but wrote guilt out of my script.

One headteacher vividly expressed her guilt about working during her daughter's babyhood and childhood:

> One of the fears I had in my mind of course was that she might be damaged by the terrible life I'd given her. And until she was quite grown up, I used to wonder whether she would be damaged. (female headteacher, quoted in Coleman, 1996a, p.328)

Women managers in general report that the disadvantages experienced by married women who try to combine a career with domestic responsibilities include: role conflict, difficulties of geographical mobility, insufficient time for both home and career, feelings of guilt (Davidson and Cooper, 1992). There is clear evidence of both guilt and role conflict for women holding senior management positions in education. Reflecting on the research findings relating to 25 primary heads, Evetts (1990) comments:

> The conflicts between work responsibilities and family responsibilities were most acute for these women during the period when their own children were very young. (p.126)

Adler *et al* (1993) in their study of senior managers in education state that 'many mothers recognize anxiety and guilt in combining the role of carer with their career.' (p.27)

Evetts (1990, p.128) reports that for the 25 heads she interviewed 'husbands had played virtually no part in the everyday care of the pre-school child'. With the exception of the small number of male head-teachers who had to take charge of the children following the death or illness of the mother, there is little evidence to indicate that the male headteachers in my survey operated differently. Guilt and role conflict were common in the responses of the women. But, for most of the men, there was an assumption that the overall responsibility was not theirs. If they felt guilty, it tended to be about the effect on the career of their spouse. In general, the care of children is clearly seen by the male head-teachers as the major responsibility of the wife and this is often reported as negotiated between them:

> My wife and I are committed to one of us being the main homemaker as vital to the stability and welfare and growth and self esteem of the children. (male headteacher)

It is also clear that both men and women believe that the ideal circumstances for the children is to be looked after in their home and often regard other arrangements as inadequate, guilt-inducing and expensive:

> It was never easy – guilt/overburden of role conflict and responsibility. (female headteacher)

It seems that it is generally the women, both wives and headteachers, who take responsibility for children (healthy or ill). Despite guilt and role conflict, Hall (1996) claims that women tend to see their combined career as wives and mothers and headteachers to be their own responsibility:

> Generally they interpreted the problem of being a working woman who is also a wife and/or mother or caregiver as their own personal problem, not one to be shared with others. (p. 58)

This view was shared by some of the female headteachers in the survey:

> As a deputy head with a young child, I felt under pressure to show extra commitment – but this came from myself largely. (female head)

This sense of responsibility extended to paying for childcare:

> You have to be prepared to spend the bulk of your earnings on good quality childcare. (female head)

> ...but expensive – I worked to pay the costs associated with having a job. (female head)

Gatenby and Humphries (1999) point out that for women who have achieved a senior position at work, this achievement is on the unstated condition that they maintain silence on some of the issues that would otherwise disturb the status quo. Certainly some of the female heads in the survey mentioned that they did not speak about domestic circumstances or problems in the work situation, preferring to distance themselves from their genuine domestic role and underplay their existence as wives and mothers: 'Never mention domestic circumstances that are problematic.' (female head)

Worries about the welfare of children were not confined to the female headteachers, but the male heads did not see the problems in terms of their own guilt:

> Concerns for our daughter having to adjust to changes in circumstances owing to child-minder variations. (male headteacher)

> Moving to different areas of the country, had to build new network – no assistance. (male headteacher)

One key question that indicates the locus of responsibility is – who looks after the child when he or she is ill?

This can be when matters come to a head. For the female headteachers, the person most often mentioned as looking after sick children was herself or her husband/partner or a combination of both. Male headteachers most often mentioned their wives, sometimes supplemented by others including himself but only two described themselves as main carer. For both men and women, the next most often mentioned categories were a grandparent, usually a grandmother, or child-minders. Friends and neighbours were mentioned less frequently. Only three of the women mentioned the possibility of paying for an agency nurse. There was a distinct difference between the genders on this question – men and women both had the same responsibilities at work but it was a different matter at home.

Several respondents commented on their good fortune in relation to the good health of their children:

> Tim has never been ill or absent from school through illness! (male head-teacher)

> The main thing was to decide that on the whole we would not be ill. I employed people as backup though. (female headteacher)

This phenomenon has been noted by Evetts (1990), commenting on 25 primary school heads:

> It was remarkable how often the women claimed that their children were seldom ill. They felt that they were lucky in that they were not ailing or sickly children. This explanation occurred so frequently that it was possible to hypothesize that working mothers might have a different perception of what constitutes illness compared with mothers who are at home. Nevertheless, these teacher-mothers were clear that in times of real sickness, their place should have been at home with their children. (p.136)

Women therefore tend to carry the major responsibility for childcare in particular. In addition, it is likely that women will bear the main responsibility for the care of aged relatives or other dependants.

Care of other dependants

The care of the elderly or other dependent relatives may lead to additional concerns and workload for the household. The headteachers were asked to indicate the nature of these responsibilities if they had them. Of the total population of female headteachers, 31.5 per cent indicated that they had such concerns, and these were slightly more prevalent amongst the over 50s, whose parents might be more likely to need help. In this group, 36.9 per cent indicated positively against 27.2 per cent of the under 50s. For those with children, 29.0 per cent indicated that they had additional domestic responsibilities. A slightly higher incidence of additional responsibilities was also true for heads of all girls' schools, where 36.6 per cent responded positively.

A smaller proportion of the men headteachers, 21.2 per cent indicated that they had responsibilities, mainly for a parent or parents, and this was true for 29.2 per cent of the over 50s and 11.8 per cent of the younger men. The range of care varied from visits and financial help to care of the housebound and dying:

> Months of weekend visits to ill and dying relatives. Holidays also taken up; breaks from work supported by sympathetic colleagues. (male head-teacher)

Most comments indicated a high degree of commitment and involvement:

> Parents, still alive in their late eighties, [are] living independently. When they are ill I do shopping and washing, also ferrying to hospital appointments and occasional gardening. (female headteacher)

> Elderly mother, in need of regular visits. (female headteacher)

However, a few commented that in their case: 'it was not arduous' and one woman headteacher had taken on the traditional male role:

> I live with my mother, mine is the financial bit. If I'm honest, she looks after me.

Neither the men nor women were asked to suggest how the care of elderly relatives might be shared between them and their partners. However, more of the women – 32 per cent – were single, separated or divorced than the men – five per cent, and care of elderly dependants appeared to be more of a responsibility for the women who were single. Also, many of the wives of the male headteachers appear to have regarded their own careers as secondary when it came to childcare so they were probably able to offer care to dependants too. A few of the male respondents implied or stated this: 'Elderly mother-in-law, led to my wife's early retirement.' (male head)

At a time when the elderly population is increasing, the care of parents and other relatives is likely to be an important factor for many of the headteachers, particularly the older half. Less than half of those surveyed reported care of the elderly, but more of these were women. For many more of the male headteachers, domestic responsibilities are at least shared, and may be largely passed to their partner.

Conclusion

The question of life/work balance for people as busy as headteachers is bound to be a difficult one. The survey responses show that the solutions to the problem include examples of negotiation and compromise between partners, and of hard decisions being made by women, particularly the younger women.

> Faced with the difficulties of combining headship, marriage and motherhood, over half of the younger women are opting to stay childless, with another relatively large group choosing to have only one child. The choices appear not to have been quite so stark for the older women who were more likely to have combined motherhood with their career. This significant change in the life choices of women over a relatively short time has not been matched in any way by the men who are headteachers.

The implications of the responses are that the men's lives are dominated by the demands of work and that, in the majority of cases, this can happen because they have the support of their wives who provide continuity to the family as the main home making partner and who often sacrifice their own career aspirations as a result. There is virtually no evidence of any change in work patterns that would achieve the balance apparently desired by our society. In the next chapter, I look further at the relationship of the headteachers with their spouses, considering the particular career strategies which might accommodate marriage and children.

Learning points for aspiring women:

- The life choices of women headteachers show that they recognise the difficulties of combining the career of headship with motherhood

- Maternity leave might keep your job open, but it does not solve problems for women trying to combine career and motherhood

- Radical changes in work patterns remain an aspiration rather than a reality.

Learning points for headteachers:

- Encourage the development of values that recognise the diversity of work patterns and more flexible ways of working

- Recognise that both men and women have family responsibilities.

5

Relationships with partners: partners and children in career planning

- Are we living in a changing world where men and women are regarded as equal in terms of work and family?

One thing is certain – in many of the homes of the headteachers surveyed there are frequent discussions about education, for 60 per cent of the female headteachers have husbands in educational occupations and the wives of 74 per cent of the male headteachers work in education, mainly as teachers. There are even headteachers who are married to each other, forty of the women and nineteen of the men. All five of the headteachers interviewed by the author (Coleman, 1996a) were married to professionals in education, two of the husbands were headteachers, two were inspectors (one retired) and the fifth was married to a teacher. 'All benefited from the fact that their partner understood the pressures they were under.' (p.327)

As we saw in the last chapter, most of the married headteachers are in dual income families but their comments show that a large number of the male headteachers and their wives gave priority to his job and that, from the domestic point of view, the men were supported by their wives, who did not work outside the home when the children were young. Over 70 per cent named wives as main childcarer. The benefits of having a supportive wife when in such a demanding job were widely recognised by the male headteachers.

Despite this, it is rare that a headteacher, male or female, can rely on a partner being *totally* available to devote the majority of her or his energy to supporting the other. About eleven per cent of male headteache wives work part-time, and only about six per cent are listed as either housewife, not working or retired. Nearly ten per cent of the husbands of the female headteachers are retired, but only three of the male partners are categorised as househusbands. Presumably most of the ten per cent of retired husbands and the 17 per cent of wives who are retired, full-time housewives or working part-time outside the home will, more or less automatically, assume the main burden of domestic tasks.

Who takes the responsibility in the home?

Who actually takes major responsibility in the home when both partners are working? Times are thought to be changing and there is an increasing expectation that men will play a part in the domestic arrangements. Therefore the possibility exists that there would be a contrast between the lives of the older and younger headteachers. The headteachers who were married or had a partner were asked to rate the extent to which they or their partner took responsibility for domestic responsibilities such as housework, shopping, cooking, washing and the organisation of holidays and social life (see Tables 5.1 and 5.2). For the 32 per cent of women and five per cent of men who did not have a partner it would be most likely that all domestic responsibility lay with them.

The figures for the headteachers in England and Wales do indicate that generally women are more likely to take the major responsibility than the men for domestic life. This is particularly true for the male headteacher households. For the households of the women headteachers, there is a greater perception of the sharing of responsibility.

Table 5.1: Sharing domestic responsibilities with husband/partner					
(Responses of women headteachers)					
	All	**under 50**	**over 50**	**children**	**no children**
More responsibility taken by the respondent	43.4	40.2	46.9	47.5	36.6
Responsibility shared 50/50	38.0	41.7	33.1	34.8	43.0
More responsibility taken by husband/partner	18.7	18.1	20.0	17.6	20.4

Women headteachers over 50, and women with children frequently took the main responsibility, reflecting the more traditional values of the older headteachers. Despite this, the largest group where responsibility is taken more by the man is amongst the over 50s probably because some are retired or semi retired.

It was women respondents without children who shared family responsibilities most equally, where the couple might have decided to be a two-career family. Alternatively this route can be taken once children are grown up. One of the headteachers I interviewed related how their dual careers meant they took joint decisions about career moves and took it in turns:

When it came to the headship, when it became obvious to my husband that that was the thing that was going to make me happy, he then said we'll move to any part of the country and we'll manage our careers that way if that's what you want to do. (female headteacher in Coleman, 1996, p.328)

Table 5.2: Sharing domestic responsibilities with wife/partner			
(Responses of men headteachers)			
	All	under 50	over 50
More responsibility taken by wife/partner	73.1	77.3	69.5
Responsibility shared 50/50	24.4	20.4	27.7
More responsibility taken by respondent	2.5	2.2	2.8

The few male headteachers (2.5 per cent) who take more responsibility is accounted for by the individuals referred to earlier, whose wife is incapacitated or has died.

Unlike the younger women headteachers, who shared with their partners a more equal division of responsibilities, the younger male headteachers are more likely to leave most domestic responsibility to their wives. The wife/partner takes major responsibility for the domestic tasks in the male headteachers' households – 73.1 per cent of cases in the survey, exactly matching findings of Davidson and Cooper (1992 p.142) who report that 73 per cent of women in the UK do nearly all the housework and that men in dual-career families have an average of hours more spare time at weekends than do their wives (Davidson Cooper, 1992, p.142). Burke and McKeen (1994) report that for career couples, the women average 30 extra days per year of shift' (p.67) work compared to their husbands or partners.

dual-career couples can afford to buy help in the home, there is still: 'much left to do, and women do the bulk of it.' (*ibid.*) Obviously there are exceptions; one of the female headteachers I interviewed, who is married to another headteacher commented that:

> Certainly at the moment the balance in terms of housework and child-care ... is heavier on my husband. I think that also at the moment, because I'm new in the job, he's doing everything he can to support me in that. (female headteacher in Coleman, 1996a, p.327)

Even where there is considerable sharing of tasks, however, the responsibility for domestic arrangements is more likely to fall on the woman. Lewis (1996, p.7) points out that:

> Initiatives such as childcare assistance enable women to act and succeed as surrogate men, putting in long hours of work and acting as though they have no primary responsibilities for family. *This does not challenge beliefs and values about traditional ways of working* and about the interdependence of work and personal lives. (my italics)

Do the women headteachers who may be acting and succeeding as surrogate men still bear the traditional responsibilities of women?

Although women generally take most responsibility for domestic arrangements including childcare, increasingly both women and men may find difficulty in

> ... co-ordinating, over time, the demands of two 'greedy institutions' (Coser 1974): the work setting and the family. This dilemma arises whenever the job is a career; that is, it requires continuous commitment, spilling over into otherwise leisure time. (Acker, 1994, p.126)

The conflict can be seen as 'a consequence of social definitions of work and family as separate and unrelated' (Lewis, 1994, p.237). The female partner within the existing social framework usually feels the problems associated with the resolution of conflicting demands more keenly. It must be remembered that my research for this book and most of that quoted here applies to an age group that is now over 40. The differences n perspective between women in their 40s and those 50 and over is iceable. It may be that women and men who aspire to leadership in ation and who are now in their 30s and 20s see things differently Blackmore (1999) found in her research on women and leader-
t:

There were clear generational differences in the storylines of these women. Women teachers in their 20s and 30s had different histories and investments in feminism than the baby boomer generation. (p.79)

Blackmore notes that some of these younger women lived with 'sensitive new age guys' (SNAGS), who presumably had a less traditional approach to apportioning domestic responsibilities.

To return to the older generation, one of the key ways in which having a partner affects one's own career is if that partner's career plans involve relocation. The traditional model has been women following men whose career normally took precedence over both family interests and the career prospects of the female partner. Cooper (1996) points out that:

Re-locating decisions, like decisions concerning initial locations, tend overwhelmingly to be in the traditional vein – in other words, to favour the husband's career. (p.95)

The headteachers who were married or had a partner were asked (see Tables 5.3 and 5.4):

Had they moved to follow their partner?

Had their partner moved to follow them?

Had they needed to operate two separate households as a result of career commitments?

Table 5.3: Moving to follow partner, or operating two households (women headteachers)

	All	under 50	over 50	children	no children
Headteachers changing jobs to follow husband/partner	37.7	30.0	47.4	41.5	31.8
Husband/partner changing jobs to follow headteacher	22.5	26.2	16.4	19.5	24.7
Operated separate households	32.0	30.0	33.3	28.5	37.3

These figures reveal a distinct age difference in attitude to the male j automatically being regarded as dominant. The women over 50 h been more likely to follow their partner/husband than those unde Among the younger women the proportion of the husband/

changing jobs to follow his wife/partner increases. There appears to be near equality in terms of whose job is considered more important. This may also apply to childless couples – the group most likely to run two separate households, possibly to avoid the potential difficulties for couples who re-locate because of the wife's career.

Couples with children have a greater incentive to try to maintain one household and they tend to follow the more traditional pattern. Women with children were more likely to change their jobs to follow their husband/partner than those with no children.

Table 5.4: Moving to follow partner or operating two households (men headteachers)			
	All	under 50	over 50
Headteachers changing Jobs to follow wife/partner	1.8	2.2	1.4
Wife/partner changing jobs to follow headteacher	49.0	48.6	49.3
Operated separate households	20.6	22.5	19.0

The statistics for the men headteachers clearly indicate that the man's job is the dominant force in the lives of the partners and this pattern does not change even among the younger groups. However, the wife and children of those who do re-locate face problems in terms of the disruption to children's education and the family's social networks. Several of the heads referred to these difficulties. One reported that: 'At the point of second deputy headship with wife and children settled in the community [I asked] – 'is it worth the upheaval?'' Both women and men felt they were tied down geographically through their families:

> When my children entered KS4, I accepted that I could only apply within a limited area. (female head)

> Towards the age of 44 [I thought I would not become a head] because we had decided not to move area as the children were settled and therefore opportunities restricted by geography. (male head)

However, one male headteacher (now divorced) did comment that his wife: 'would rather have slit her throat' than changed her job to follow

Considering the traditional division of labour operating in most of the male headteacher households, the small number of men headteachers re-locating to follow their wife is not surprising. Cooper, (1996, p.95) refers to the belief that men who do not conform to the expectation that they will be mobile are seen in terms of traditional values as 'lacking in professional commitment.'

This picture emerges of two distinct gender-driven patterns of arrangements for households. In one, the women headteachers, particularly the younger ones, were operating in households usually with the expectation of two, relatively equal careers, and where re-locating was possible for either partner to take up a new job. Although domestic responsibilities were seldom equally shared, neither were they allocated purely on a traditional basis.

In the other pattern, common among the men headteachers and their wives, there is little evidence of such changes. The man's job is the key factor in deciding the location of the family and, in the younger families in particular, there is minimal sharing of domestic responsibilities. The couples largely operate a traditional system. Indeed they may even aspire to the wife staying at home. One of the men commented that childcare was: 'very difficult at times. I would have preferred my wife to be at home [but it was] not economical.'

The survey of managers undertaken by the Institute of Management (Charlesworth, 1997) showed a similar pattern where women still tended to take the main responsibility, but more sharing took place in the dual career families:

> Over half the women managers took sole responsibility for most of the domestic tasks;
>
> Around 70 per cent of the male managers left responsibility for household matters to their wives
>
> Where the financial contribution to the household income was more equal men were more likely to share in the domestic tasks. (pp.41-43)

Career strategies

In Chapter Three, I focused on the career plans of the headteachers without including the variables of marriage and children. I outlined the phases of career: preparation and anticipation; establishment; advancement or development and finally acquiring headship – the 'peak' of the career. I now look at the careers of the women and men in the survey considering the interweaving of family responsibilities with their career.

Although marriage, family and children have enormous impact on all individuals, the major impact is still on women. Building on the data from the previous section however, suggests a spectrum of experience that can be divided into three main models.

> The most traditional model is where the wife takes virtually all the domestic responsibility, as many of the wives of the men headteachers do. The second model is of the woman having a career while also taking the traditional role. This seems to apply to at least some of the older women headteachers. Finally there is the possibility of a more equal distribution of responsibilities within a dual career family exhibited among some of the younger women, some of whom may have decided not to have children.

All these models focus on the lives of the women, because it is they who generally have to interweave the responsibilities and pleasures of family and the demands and challenges of career. Four of the men headteachers were single parents or had wives incapacitated in some way, so took on the 'female' role. There are also three men, married to female head-teachers who termed themselves house-husbands. But most of what follows concerns the interweaving of family and career responsibilities by the women headteachers and the wives of the men headteachers.

To develop these models further, some of the career theories of Evetts (1990 and 1994) are helpful. Evetts (1994) identified a number of career strategies of women teachers. One is the 'single career' where possibilities include that the person remains single or becomes single due to death, divorce or separation. This model of a single career would apply to five per cent of the men headteachers and 32 per cent of the women. Evetts (1994) also points out, however, that a single career may be the joint decision of a couple, where one (usually the wife) opts to support the other and has no career. This might include those wives of the men headteachers who choose not to work or work part-time. One of the male headteachers wrote that:

My wife felt confident of her decision and what she was doing, until our younger one finished at university and finally left a year or two later. It is only during these last two or three years until my retirement that she wonders occasionally if she is under-employed and a little less purposeful than she likes to be.

A variation on the one person career strategy may be the 'accommodated' career which: 'will have involved balancing personal and teaching responsibilities over the course of the working life' (Evetts, 1990, p.69). Those (usually) women adopting this approach may reject promotion so as to minimise potential for role conflict. Careers of this type certainly were evident among the wives of the male headteachers:

Wife happy to give up work and return to work on part-time basis whilst children young. (male headteacher)

My wife has had to give up her career for mine. She now can't get back in because she is too expensive. (male headteacher)

Many of the male heads put their success down to having a wife happy and willing to take a greater share of domestic responsibilities.

The one-person-career strategy can be a deliberate choice, to avoid the difficulties that marriage and family can bring to a career. None of the female headteachers in the survey commented on this, but one female head interviewed in Ozga (1993) reacted against the potential tensions of dual career strategies:

I've anxieties about able women colleagues who won't try for posts because they're sensitive that their husbands' feelings might be hurt. I believe that they shouldn't put careers on back burners just to be supportive. That kind of thing makes me cross because, though it may ensure domestic harmony at the time, later it may cause professional frustration and resentment. (Maureen Sedgewick in Ozga, 1993, p.55)

An alternative strategy allows each partner has a commitment to career, but where (usually) the woman makes some adjustment to accommodate the family. This approach is adopted by women who want career, marriage and children and have to find a way to 'have it all'. The main strategies that can be adopted are: postponement; modification or balancing (Evetts, 1994).

Postponement strategy

In the case of deferred promotion, family goals are the main priority in the early part of the career. Some of the women who adopt this strategy may have come into teaching later after they have had their children. Inevitably, they tend to achieve their headship posts when older than average, and their career takes on more significance in later life. This strategy seems to have been more common with the older female head-teachers, who were also much more likely than the younger ones to have taken a longer career break to have children. A quarter of them had taken such a break (average 2.5 years) as against under five per cent of the younger women. About a quarter of the women who commented on childcare mentioned delaying their career until the children were at least in school:

> I stayed at home. I ran a playgroup and they came too. (female head-teacher)

> I stayed at home for several years in part-time jobs – I nearly missed out on headship because of my advanced age! (female headteacher)

There is also evidence of deferred promotion amongst the wives of the men headteachers.

> [My] wife put her career on 'hold' until younger child was eight – was recently appointed to headship (male headteacher)

In their research on 150 highly successful women educational adminis-trators in the USA, Gupton and Appelt Slick (1996) found that 67 per cent identified problems at the point of balancing a family and career. As a result, many of them chose to take a postponement strategy and delay their career.

Modification strategy

An alternative way of looking at career strategies is to consider modification of the career. The additional responsibility of caring for dependent relatives such as parents was experienced by about a third of all the headteachers over 50, a quarter of the women under 50 and twelve per cent of the men under 50. Whilst this was not always identi-fied as a heavy responsibility, it might well be a factor in modification strategy for some of the heads and their wives. Career modification may be more common among women than men because of what Acker (1999) terms 'accidents'. In following the careers of the women teachers at 'Hillview' primary school, she recounts the incidents of illness, miscarriage and death that impinged on their careers and summarises her view:

> Careers are provisional kaleidoscopic constructions, made up of everyday events and interchanges, surrounded by dimly perceived structural constraints and characterized by change... (Acker, 1999, p.166)

Gatenby and Humphries (1999) also comment on the importance of aspects of women's lives that are not taken into account in the normal discourse on career and career planning, such as abortion, miscarriage and infertility, noting that they are taboo subjects, yet have enormous impact on individual lives.

Domestic circumstances were indicated as influencing or modifying career by twice as many women as men in my survey, particularly women over 50, who were significantly more likely than their younger colleagues to rate this as an influence. Not surprisingly the group that mentioned domestic circumstances most were those with children. Some of the major domestic circumstances itemised as affecting the career plan include divorce and widowhood, but more everyday matters had also affected professional life:

> I returned to full time in 1976 and was happy at this stage to aim at head of year. Like Topsy, 'responsibilities' grew. In that school deputy headship came up. I didn't apply, but it made me realise it was something I could do and wanted! Plus mother had moved in to run the house! (female headteacher)

Another female headteacher in the survey indicated what had spurred her on in her career planning:

> A personal crisis meant I was in it for the duration and that decided me to go forward.

Careers may have been subject to modification by the 37.7 per cent of the female married headteachers who indicated that they had changed jobs at some time to follow their husband or partner and the 49 per cent of wives of male headteachers who had done so. For the husbands who had followed their wives, the strategy might also be described as balancing.

Balancing strategy

Evidence of the balancing strategy comes from the changing pattern evident among the younger female headteachers, where the husbands or partners are almost as likely to follow them in a career move as the wives are to follow their husbands. There is also much greater sharing of domestic responsibilities (see tables 5.1 and 5.3). It was also evident among the headteachers I interviewed where one husband had actually moved three times to follow the career progress of his wife.

Throughout this discussion, there has been an underlying assumption that the male model of career is the norm and it is to that norm that career women aspire. For some women as well as men, the overall commitment may be to career success identified in this more traditional way. Evetts (1990) terms this the antecedent career, where a woman is highly committed to her working career right from the beginning and does not deviate from it.

The 'male' model of career

In such a career, work takes precedence and a woman who adopts this route is likely to have no children. This appears to be true for about half of the female headteachers. Whether or not they made a conscious decision not to have children, significantly fewer of the younger female headteachers have no children, suggesting that at least some are choosing work in preference to having a family. A model of career has been identified by Osipow (1995, quoted in White, 2000, p.170) inasmuch as a model for women exists today, consisting 'of early career entry, a brief interruption for family obligations and a return to the workforce for the rest of the lifespan'. A study of 48 successful British businesswomen (White, 2000) mapped their career paths, identifying that they rejected the concept of the housewife role in their 20s and established their careers between the ages of 25 and 32. During the transition phase of their mid to late 30s their 'awareness of the biological clock' (p.167) increased. They resolved this either by having a child or children and taking minimum maternity leave or else moving through a period of regret at not having children to rationalising their decision in their 40s. Such a pattern was probably followed by many of the women in my study. Certainly, many of the younger women had taken minimum maternity leave or else had chosen to have no children or only one child. One of the younger women reported:

> As my children were planned and arrived in late June and August, I had minimal time off and was able to return in September both times.

The impact of the introduction of maternity leave is shown by the different pattern of career breaks for the under and over 50s indicated in Table 5.5. Those under 50 are significantly more likely to have taken a maternity break and significantly less likely than their older women colleagues to have taken a longer break to have children.

Table 5.5: Career breaks for female headteachers under and over 50

	under 50 %	over 50 %
had a career break	37.8	56.7
maternity leave	21.5	13.4
longer break (children)	4.5	26.9

Career breaks that were not for children were most often for secondment to gain a qualification. Men took career breaks mainly for that reason and none reported a career break associated with childcare.

Table 5.6: Career breaks for male headteachers under and over 50

	all	under 50	over 50
Having a career break	10.1	5.4	14.1

Although many of the women headteachers, particularly the younger ones may have adopted a 'male' model of career, it does not mean that career success need be judged only in those terms.

The 'female' or subjective view of career

An alternative to career success in 'male' terms is what Evetts (1990) calls the 'subjective career'. By this she means a female teacher's view of her career as successful where, for example, she has managed to combine motherhood with successful classroom teaching:

> The concept of the subjective career is concerned with how individuals have actually experienced their working lives and the meaning they attach to their work and careers. (p.63)

These women are taking a holistic view of their careers, scarcely differentiating the world of work from their domestic responsibilities:

> The responsibility for the maintenance of the marital home and, particularly, the physical care and emotional well being of young children, is seen to lie with the women. So, whereas men can and do talk about their career as something totally separate and distinct from their personal and family lives, for women career goals and personal ambitions are more intimately intertwined and interrelated. (*ibid.* p.64)

Careers of this type may well have been followed by many of the wives of the male headteachers. Intriguingly, the 'male' concept of a successful career as judged only in terms of power, status and position is being modified with regard to men as well as women in the business world:

> Workers, it is argued, no longer expect jobs for life, but do expect opportunities for self-development. This is usually interpreted in terms of employability but, given the interdependence between work and family, also encapsulates opportunities to balance work and family in an optimal way. (Lewis, 1996, p.3)

Female career models

The headteachers I questioned reveal a fair amount about themselves, their plans and the parts played by their spouses. They are successful individuals who, although they did not all plan each stage, have generally made a fairly structured progress along a defined career path to a post that is extremely demanding. The glimpses of the lives of the wives of the male headteachers reveal an alternative type of career model that may be considered traditional or may be experienced as subjectively successful.

The headteachers themselves have gone through phases of preparation; establishment, advancement and acquisition. However, those with family commitments have had to make decisions, particularly at the establishment and advancement stages. For the male headteachers this has meant handing over large portions of responsibility for home and children to their wives, probably at the cost of an optimal balance between work and family. For their wives it has largely meant adopting a traditional role or an 'accommodated' career subjugated to the career of their husband.

The female headteachers show a shift in attitude depending on age. The younger female heads and their husbands are more likely to be living with a non-traditional model of career that assumes that family life is merely a brief interruption and that career is central to both partners' lives. One might say that they are operating a more balanced strategy for managing joint careers. The older female heads and their husbands are more likely to have adopted a mixed career model, the wife having, in effect, a joint role of successful career woman who also takes the major responsibility for family and domestic life. Some might see this as the worst of both worlds and the classic example of what has been termed the double or even the triple shift: the woman does a job, runs the house and also looks after children (Acker, 1994).

In every group, men and women, but the older women heads in particular, there were some who, through divorce, separation or widowhood, were single parents who therefore took entire responsibility for career and home. Also there were some, including members of religious orders, who remained single. Among women with family responsibilities, however, the following models emerge:

traditional/subjective
mixed mode
changing/balanced

Table 5.7 Female career models

	Traditional/ subjective	Mixed Mode	Changing
Who?	wives of headteachers	older women headteachers	younger women headteachers and their partners
children?	Yes	Yes	less than half have children
career break?	Yes	Yes	Minimal maternity leave
main childcare responsibility?	wife	woman has responsibility, uses childminder	more likely to share responsibility
main career strategy?	single or subjective career or accommodated career	postponed, moderated or balanced	'male' model or balanced
domestic responsibility?	mainly with wives	more often with women, some sharing	more evidence of sharing
moving to follow husband?	Yes, common	Yes, fairly common	almost equal with husband

Conclusion

The 'changing' model of career for the younger women headteachers and their partners represents a new development. However, alongside this model, the *status quo* still operates. The traditional model can be seen in the lives of the men headteachers' wives. In this model the women have the opportunity to live a family life while their husbands may be missing out on much of it, but these wives subordinate their careers to those of their husbands.

The older women headteachers were more likely to take several years' career break and possibly work part-time while their children were young. However, many of the younger women are either not having children or taking minimal maternity leave. Despite some changes it does not appear that the 'male' model of career is being challenged, or that an alternative model that would offer a better life/work balance to women and men is becoming widely established.

> Women have been entrapped by male norms and they are accommodating to these norms rather than challenging the rules of the game. (White, 2000, p.173)

Learning points for aspiring women:
- There is more than one model of successful career.

- Dual career families are now more likely to adopt a balanced career strategy.

- Younger female headteachers are more likely to opt for a 'male' model of career and are not providing an alternative model.

Learning points for headteachers:
- Women may adopt a variety of career strategies

- Men and women can both take responsibility for children and domestic life.

6

Stereotypes: macho leadership or niceness and tears?

- Will I be up against institutionalised views that make my career progress difficult?

- Will I have credibility as a leader and manager if I combine motherhood and a career?

- How will men react to being managed by a woman?

- Will I have to be seen to lead 'like a man' if I am going to be considered a good headteacher?

Most of the chapters so far have started with one or more of the bullet point questions which opened the book. This chapter deals with those that include the most common stereotypes that exist around the area of women and men in leadership. The nature of these stereotypes which pervade the thinking of both sexes (Schein, 1994) means that there are even more questions at the start of this chapter. The stereotypes cause barriers to career progress and centre round the unthinking belief that there is a 'natural order' – male leadership and female subordination. Allied to this are preconceived ideas stereotyping male and female leadership style (central to the discussion in Chapter Seven).

The stereotypes implicit in the questions above identify women as less worthy or qualified than men to lead and manage. The 'socially constructed meaning of gender' (Schmuck, 1996, p.350) stereotypically confines women to subordinate roles and identifies them with the domestic. In turn, the domestic arena is seen as inferior to the public arena – the 'proper' place of men.

Gender stereotypes make career progress difficult

Chapters Two and Three examined the relative difficulties women experience in attaining a headship. Once in post, the difficulties associated with gender do not disappear. One of the major impacts of gender on work was the probability that the women would experience some feelings of isolation. In fact it is not unusual for all new heads to feel isolated. One of the main benefits of mentoring identified by new heads was the reduction of that isolation (Bush *et al* 1996). However, women may experience this feeling of isolation more than their male colleagues. As noted, women headteachers are spread unevenly around the country. In London, where at least 50 per cent of the secondary heads are women, and where the ILEA heritage of equal opportunities still has effect, isolation is not the problem that it is for women in shire counties. The five headteachers interviewed (Coleman, 1996a) were the only women headteachers in one shire county and commented on the importance of meeting others, particularly when they first began. One of them stated that her main source of support was 'close head colleagues – although there aren't many of those and they do tend to be women, I must admit' (*ibid.* p.324). The comments in the survey about the isolation felt by female headteachers were very emotive evoking additional comments and accompanying letters from some respondents. It seems that many of them welcomed the opportunity to give vent to their feeling. One stated that she was 'very isolated as a female Head. I could write pages.'

The isolation they reported related also to networking and meetings of other headteachers, the LEA or unions:

> A very 'male' attitude exists at headteachers' level in the area, it is apparent at heads' meetings. The LEA (which I greatly value) is very male dominated in many respects.

> A LEA officer (senior) tickled my neck once in County Hall! He didn't do that to any of the others (all men). I intend to one day point this out to him but I'll choose my moment.

> Secondary Heads' meetings in that authority were painful in the extreme at first, an old boys' club of really unreconstructed men in waistcoats – I felt completely marginalized. But they too were capable of change...

Women operating in a male dominated culture, working for example in groups of secondary headteachers, may find some difficulty with the dynamics of committee processes, which tend to exemplify male styles of communication. Reporting on management development courses, Gold (1996) identifies the following findings:

Males tend to dominate meetings, typically taking well over half of speaking time

Men tend to speak for several minutes, whilst women tend to 'make short, succinct comments'

Women tend to be ignored more than men are, by the chair and other committee members

The contributions of women tend not to be acknowledged

Women may be inhibited by the sometimes aggressive nature of debate

Women are more likely to lack confidence in addressing the meeting.

(adapted from Gold, 1996, p.426)

Responses in the survey certainly indicated experience of this kind. In one case a woman headteacher reported that:

Secondary Heads' meetings are always 80 per cent men, and bullying is commonplace. I have been subjected to extremely insulting verbal abuse from a 'colleague' and no one said a word!

And one of the female heads interviewed (Coleman, 1996a, p.329) commented on a meeting she had recently attended:

I spoke on a number of occasions, I think very much to the point. And one man actually turned to the person he was with and said 'who is that?' And if was very much a matter of 'what right has she got to be speaking?'

The female headteachers noted also that women find it difficult to be accepted in the 'old boy' network. In the survey of men and women managers undertaken by the Institute of Management (Charlesworth, 1997), the most important career barrier identified by the women was 'old boys' network' followed by 'prejudice of colleagues'. Where men hold all or most of the senior positions, male culture may effectively exclude women from entering. At its most extreme, women may find themselves effectively barred from potentially influential meetings and institutions, such as male dominated clubs. Although this is more common and relevant in commerce, it may also occur within the world of education. A female American superintendent reports how she paid for one of her male principals to join the Rotary Club so that she could always go as his guest: 'in order to meet face-to-face and shake hands with the community power-brokers' (Bell, 1995, p.300). Delamont (1990) identifies that British women aspiring to headship may also be disadvantaged

> ...if promotion in school teaching depends in part on meeting heads, councillors and LEA officials at the Freemasons, the rugby club, the Conservative party headquarters, or the golf club. (p.88)

One of the male headteachers in the survey commented negatively on the overtly male atmosphere that might exclude women and men who did not subscribe to the dominant mode of behaviour:

> the use of male based vocabulary in meetings ... hence 'male bonding' type atmosphere at meetings.

His sensitivity is relatively rare in the responses. Most men and a minority of the women are to some extent unconscious of the messages of male exclusivity that are being received by most women heads and by other women in leadership roles.

Women are in the 'wrong' place

One of the clearest messages to emerge from the responses of the headteachers is that most of the women know they are in an exposed position as leaders. Consequently they are more likely than men to feel that they have to prove themselves and believe that they have to work harder than men to earn their place.

Most headteachers felt that they had to prove their worth as a manager but the men generally considered gender not to be an issue, and that proving your worth as a manager was simply something that went with the job. Some remarked that they could not understand why this question was linked with their gender. As men, they had not questioned their right to be in a leadership position. One of the male heads said:

> You have to prove your worth at whatever level if you are to obtain promotion – it is not a matter of gender.

However, only a small minority of the women felt that gender was irrelevant to the matter of proving your worth, and most of their comments were about the stereotyped views automatically attached to a woman in a leadership position. The women who reacted most strongly about proving their worth were those most obviously labelled as female because they were married and had children and were heads of co-ed schools. Being perceived as responsible for a family helps to shape stereotypes about women and what is appropriate work for them. Shakeshaft (1989) concluded from her research findings that:

> Thus home and family responsibilities provide obstacles for women in administration in two ways: the woman not only must effectively juggle all of her tasks, she must also contend with the bulk of male school board presidents and superintendents who erroneously believe that not only is she unable to manage the balancing act but that it is inappropriate for her to even attempt it. (p.113)

The headteachers least likely to be worried about issues of gender worked in situations where their gender would have been perceived as less relevant: they were the single, childless and/or heads of girls' schools. However, even the latter commented on having to prove themselves if they wanted to become head of a co-ed school. Although very few of the men linked the idea of proving themselves to their gender, the one who came close to it was one of only two male heads of a girls' school:

> I felt I had to prove my worth, but not because I was a man; rather because I wanted to do a good job. As a male head in a girls' school I was conscious that a particular style would be appropriate.

What was uppermost in the minds of the women thinking about proving themselves as heads was the need to break away from the stereotypes associated with women in management, and particularly to overcome the domestic role stereotyping of female headteachers. Some consequently felt the need to underplay the domestic part of their lives and either deliberately minimise domesticity or display their overt commitment to their work:

> As a Deputy I had to make a conscious effort not to do what was expected, e.g. always make the coffee for the (otherwise all male) SMT meeting. It was quite difficult ... as they demonstrated such a high level of planned incompetence, but we got there in the end.

> Work extra long hours, not take time off for my own health or my children's, and take on extras like conference work.

There is little if any recognition of the potential value of actually having children in terms of management and what Ozga (1993, p.2) refers to as: 'the complex, varied and rich experience of women's lives that develops their particular management styles and capacities.' She makes the point this experience is generally perceived as low-status and value-less.

The employers of one head did recognise that she had probably bene-fited from a career break to look after children:

> So I went from my eight years of maternity leave, [four sons] back into teaching as a deputy head. This was an unusual progression. And I think I found the one job in the country where the people appointing me placed great value on the fact that I had spent eight years at home bringing up my family and they saw that as adding significantly to what I could offer. (Mary Marsh, in Ribbins, 1997, p.134)

Other female heads in the survey recognised the benefits that ex-perience at home brings to their career in school:

> As a mum as well, I can see issues from a parental viewpoint. [Headship involves] similar skills to running a busy household with five in the family.

> Most teachers are women, most heads of department at my last school were women (married and mothers), and we understand the demands of family/parenthood/career and shared and supported each other.

Women may well perceive the benefits to their management skills from the experience of running a household but men are less likely to do so. In general, the identification of women with domestic tasks and child-care does not increase their chances of promotion but seems to enhance the essentialist stereotype that places women as 'carers' rather than managers and leaders.

Some of the male headteachers surveyed were also aware of stereo-typical attitudes amongst their staff about women having domestic res-ponsibilities:

> There is an assumption (often unspoken) that it is more important for men to have a career.

> Childcare – women's responsibility.

Several comments were made about visitors automatically presuming that the headteacher was the secretary or of some lower status:

> I have worked as a head with male deputies – it is always assumed I am
> the secretary or at best a deputy by first-time callers who don't know the
> school. (female headteacher)

One man commented that:

> I worked as a deputy with a woman head and on more than one occasion
> when we attended conferences together it was assumed I was the head.

Women in leadership roles are also believed to have to be better than a
man to get the job. This view was actually endorsed by a large number
of the heads. Over 20 per cent of the heads who responded said as
much, and this view was also taken by the heads interviewed (Coleman,
1996b). The picture that emerges is of beleaguered women desperately
trying to operate as superwomen because the odds are stacked against
their being there in the first place.

- They are expected to work harder:

  > Working harder and being more efficient than anyone else. (female
  > head)

  > 'always felt that I had to be first into school and last to leave. (I still
  > do!) (female head)

- They are expected to work better:

  > You have to be seen to be twice as good as male colleagues. (female
  > head)

- They are expected to please everyone 'by working harder than
  anyone.'

  > ...juggling the demands of home with school and trying to do the
  > 'right thing' by everyone. (female head)

- They are expected to give birth in off-duty hours:

  > Providing superhuman commitment, energy and hours either side of
  > maternity leaves! (female head)

Many referred to the long hours of work that they were prepared to
undertake. The need to work harder is linked to stereotypes about the
way women work and manage and the expectation that they will live up
to or even exceed the qualities expected of a male head:

> Not allowed mistakes, not allowed to be decisive – considered only a male quality.

> Not allowed to make mistakes, judged more harshly than men, more is expected of you, you have to be efficient and nice.

> Women need to be twice as calm as their male counterparts and demonstrate their toughness in difficult situations and in a crisis.

The need to prove themselves was keenly felt by the three female respondents who were black or Asian:

> As a black Muslim woman I had to do more than that [i.e. prove herself as a woman manager].

> Both as a woman and a black person.

> On my third day of headship I had to cope with a very irate member of staff who took great pains to inform me that I had only got my job because I was an Asian female.

In a major study of black and ethnic women managers, Davidson (1997) found one of the problems most frequently cited by those interviewed could be summarised as: 'having to prove oneself more than white women and the pressure of having to sell oneself constantly' (p.39).

The exposure of women as heads seems to give others a right to be critical and negative about them that is rarely applied to men. No matter what the circumstances of the individual woman, there appears to be a stereotype to match. Munro (1998, p.3) points out that: 'Images of schoolteachers include the spinster, the school ma'am, the old maid and the mother- teacher. These stereotypes represent contradictory images.' Such contradictory stereotypes were clearly evident in the survey responses. The following four comments, all from women headteachers in my survey, illustrate this nicely, and relate to the style of management and the sexuality of the individual. First, the expectation of a 'soft' and inadequate management style:

> The assumption was that you will be a female stereotype – keep changing one's mind, can't handle difficult male pupils etc.

Then where a woman is recognised as successful:

> the suggestion that career women are cold, hard and single-minded.

Next is the identification of the female with domesticity:

> As head of department, I was the only woman at that level. It was hard to change attitudes: I was expected to take minutes, make the tea and have nothing interesting to say.

Finally, stereotypical prejudice about an unmarried woman:

> More a question of little bits of prejudice against single woman role. Rumours seemed to vary: I'm assumed to be either a promiscuous heterosexual or a latent homosexual.

There are simply not the equivalent sets of stereotypes about men. It is as though the normality of male leadership and the relative abnormality of female leadership sanctions criticism of women heads and aspiring heads but not of men. However, there were occasional remarks from both women and men that macho and highly formal styles of leadership were identified as male and, moreover, seen to be outdated. One of the interviewed heads thought, for example, that:

> There are differences between men and women in the job. Women are more likely to own up when things are going wrong. ... One of the things I don't like is pomposity and status. (Coleman, 1996b, p.172)

She was clearly implying that it was men who were inclined to pomposity and worries about status. But this was one of very few instances where men were negatively stereotyped by the women respondents. Male heads occasionally showed resentment that they were subject to gender stereotyping:

> Some women think male heads are insensitive. (male head)

> Assumption that males do not share domestic responsibilities. (male head)

The main gender-related problem for the women heads was the resentment felt by men and some women about females in a leadership role, the underlying belief that leadership is inappropriate for women.

Resentment of women as leaders

Once established as headteachers, the women were strongly aware that men found difficulty in dealing with female leaders. Men headteachers were also aware of this stereotype:

> When first appointed as a head of physics with a female head of science it was apparent that they expected me to resent having a woman above me. (male headteacher)

Many comments express 'difficulties with the concept of woman as a boss'. Some were more specific:

> I inherited a school with a good number of staff who didn't want a female head. The secretary and caretaker threatened to resign, some male teachers made it clear they didn't want a woman telling them what to do. (female head)

Difficulties were associated particularly with age, with working with colleagues who had been passed over for promotion and with gaining credence among a predominantly male senior management team:

> When I took over here it was obvious that one man in particular found it very difficult to have a female head. I actually had to tackle him at the senior management meeting because he was looking to heaven, doing all sorts of things. (female headteacher in Coleman, 1996b, p.320)

The black or Asian female headteachers had additional difficulties with senior management:

> A greater willingness to question decisions and to doubt my abilities, but ... both sexism and racism apply here. (female headteacher)

The female heads studied by Hall reported that openness with colleagues was more difficult when the colleague was male, although differences tended to be blamed by the headteachers on different 'chemistry' rather than gender assumptions (Hall, 1996, p.190). Quantitative research carried out in the mid 1980s with a large national sample of high school teachers and principals in the USA also identified potential difficulties when women lead the men:

> It is clear that the daily practices of principals are seen quite differently by men and women teachers, and those differences are magnified when we consider the principal's gender. A strong and consistent finding from the study is that women teachers feel empowered when working in environments where their direction comes from women leaders, and male teachers do not. (Riehl and Lee, 1996, p.892)

Several hypotheses are put forward for why working with women may make men uncomfortable. One is resistance to unfamiliarity, since leaders are stereotypically male, another the way women leaders tend towards participatory management – which men may see as a threat to their autonomy as teachers – and finally that:

...an in-group bias might also prejudice men against women leaders. Men have been well served in a system where their own gender dominates the principalship. (Riehl and Lee, 1996, p.893)

Working with women leaders in some cases may advantage women but the dominant cultural influences mean that leadership is generally equated with maleness.

Different ways of leading

The management and leadership of the male and female heads were perceived as very stereotyped. One head stated that: 'some staff wanted as Head a 'big man who shouted' – I'm the opposite'. In general the prevailing stereotype was linked to the idea of tough leadership that would only be embodied in a man and that women in management would be too soft and unable to cope.

Some governors assumed when I was first appointed to a headship that I might be 'too nice' – they assumed that only aggression could change opinion.

The chair of governors frequently praises my 'decisive firm approach', because it was like his, i.e. masculine.

I had to demonstrate that I could take tough decisions when needed e.g. staff discipline.

Male governors, especially in the past, have expected tears or illness or whatever!

(female headteachers)

The assumption is that there is only one correct way to manage – a 'male' way – and that showing emotions and being nice had no place when it came to leading a school.

One male headteacher observed that stereotypes about women were; 'innumerable, based on height, stopping fights, leading older men etc. etc.' The assumption that women could not deal with what may be perceived as the male domain extended to other specific issues such as finance and buildings:

There has been a presumption that my husband helps with the finance. (female headteacher)

> Tendency among some senior staff to steer women away from harder edged areas such as the budget. (male headteacher)

> We have had major building [plant] problems – LEA officers patronise (or tried!) (female headteacher)

These stereotypes generated a belief among some of the female headteachers that they were especially 'put to the test' as women, by being given roles that might have been considered hard for a woman and then being watched to see whether they met the challenge. High amongst these tasks was the ability to deal with discipline, particularly the disciplining of 'big boys'.

> Discipline – I have never had a problem with discipline, but the staff were watching me to see if I could 'handle' disaffected or disruptive pupils initially. I was 'on trial' particularly with my response to discipline issues. (female headteacher)

> 'Macho' style ability to do any task was required when I was a Deputy Head – e.g. I had to stop fights, snowballing, and deal with trespass. (female headteacher)

> As a deputy head – having more difficult and challenging tasks than two fellow male deputy heads. (female headteacher)

> Given staff absence cover from day one of my deputy's job, with no assistance, not knowing the staff or curriculum well, to fill in the last six weeks of the summer term before starting my proper job spec. in September. Told later it was a test to see if I would survive. (female headteacher)

Most of the heads of both sexes perceived that views were in general traditionalist – women were seen as weaker and less able than men. One spin-off was that a minority saw women as having too much power.

Reaction to women's promotion – the 'backlash' effect
A few of the female headteachers indicated that colleagues felt that the pendulum had swung too far in favour of women, even when this meant that men and women were simply equal in number.

> Comments that equal numbers of male/female interviewees was sexist, and that women are only interviewed to have the right 'PC' balance.

> Some feeling in my current school that the management structure is too heavily female, when it is actually 50/50.

In addition, the view was expressed that it was easier for women than men to get certain jobs:

> Initially some staff thought I'd been appointed because I'm a woman. It's largely been overcome.

Men headteachers also made such comments:

> Male staff sometimes think I only promote women.

They showed that the culture of the workplace does sometimes vary from the traditional view that men should be in charge:

> When working for 15 years in East London, political correctness/feminist lobby influenced appointments and shape of curriculum – this may not have been wholly bad.

However, male headteachers also made negative comments concerning the behaviour of women in work, saying, for example, that they had more time off than men, or that some male teachers considered that women: 'did not pull their weight'.

The male headteachers in the survey were much less likely than the women to report awareness of sexist attitudes. Two thirds of women but only about a third of the men said that they had been aware of sexist attitudes. However, the sexist attitudes the men were commenting on concerned what they had observed of the experience of women and was usually qualified by a belief that things are improving:

> Of course I have been aware of sexist attitudes amongst some colleagues sometimes – but these attitudes no longer predominate. (male head)

A male culture in education

Although women numerically dominate education, the prevailing culture in co-educational secondary education is likely to be male. One conference, with contributions from many European countries including the UK, the USA and Australia, came to a general conclusion:

> Several [other] speakers and written contributions described the masculine culture in educational institutions as a major barrier to women seeking promotion. (Ruijs, 1993, p.561)

Mac an Ghaill (1994) observed the gender politics of the British staffroom:

There was little awareness among the Old Collectivist [term refers to their union support] male teachers of the gender structuring of public arenas, such as the staffroom, that highlighted the power of masculinity as an institutional force, operating to marginalize and exclude women, while privileging the masculine perspective. Furthermore, there was little acknowledgement of the predatory heterosexual environment of staffroom, classroom and playground, that female teachers and students frequently recounted to me. (p.29)

Headteachers in my survey were aware of a masculine culture operating in certain staffrooms, sometimes linked to gender 'jokes' and even bullying:

General male chauvinism in current staffroom – now very much diminished if not banished. (male head)

The pervasive male culture may be enhanced by what Cunnison (1989) identified as 'gender joking' provoked by the competitive relationship between teachers over promotion, where gender is an important principle of social differentiation. The jokes tended to focus on issues of femininity and domesticity:

Gender joking is almost entirely initiated by men. It is men defining women at work in sexual, domestic or maternal terms, terms which detract from their image as professionals. As such it is a put-down, a way of controlling and subordinating women ... and one mechanism among others which militates against their promotion.' (p.166)

One male head in the survey referred to the 'simple humour that sometimes hides a more sinister reality'. And a female head commented 'remarks at meetings – when is a jocular remark not a jocular remark?'

Gender joking impinges on what some perceive as sexual harassment – a subject touched on in Chapter Three. In a study of 35 women educational leaders in the USA (Hill and Ragland, 1995) only seven replied 'no' to the question 'have you ever been sexually harassed?' although the responses did include some like 'not really' or 'yes ... no big deal,' and 'by some standards' which:

... may indicate a form of passive acceptance or denial of a very insidious phenomenon that many women leaders experience. (Hill and Ragland, 1995, p.108)

Davidson and Cooper (1992) report that in an in-depth study of 60 female managers in the UK, 52 per cent of the sample reported sexual harassment at work. They note that:

> Sexual harassment is, indeed, a more extreme form of the behaviour that goes on each day between male and female managers ... at work. Sexuality is frequently used in one guise or another by both men and women as a method of career advancement, to influence decisions at work or to 'put down' overly ambitious colleagues. (p.112)

While the term sexual harassment may connote a serious matter which could lead to dismissal, the term 'sexist' or 'sexism' may be used in conjunction with the male culture of the staffroom, or the viewpoint of those responsible for selection and promotion. Female headteachers encounter many reminders of the fact that they are female in what is generally perceived to be a male job and if she is also black, she faces even more possibilities of criticism and stereotyping:

> So I had to work hard – doubly hard to prove that I was a good headteacher, a good, black headteacher, a good, black female headteacher. I felt I was in a glass cage all the time being watched. (Vasanthi Rao, in Mortimore and Mortimore, 1991 p.81)

Sexual harassment is probably reported more in industry (Davidson and Cooper, 1992) than in education. However, incidents were reported by heads in the survey. One male headteacher reported two specific incidents. In one a 'male senior member of staff was patronising towards young female staff – sufficient to warrant complaint and verbal warning from me'.

A female headteacher reported a situation, which indicated a case of bullying. Writing about experiences of sexism from colleagues, she reported:

> Not recently. In the school where I was deputy all female staff were put on top of the lockers in the staff room. Had to cope. A sort of rite of passage. After that – fine.

Some of the female headteachers commented on inappropriate language on the part of male headteachers and staff: 'a headteacher (male) colleague used to say 'my dear'...' and 'doing the timetable on a computer for the first time with the male deputy who used to call me 'lover'.

In addition, some of the female headteachers described encountering patronising attitudes and remarks from colleagues, governors and even men who were their subordinates:

> Sometimes patronised or flirted with (by governors).

> Some males similar in age but junior in the hierarchy try to patronise.

Women as well as men were occasionally seen as patronising or vindictive:

> Put down by men who did not wish me to open my mouth in staff meetings (only men could speak), obscene jokes about me by male members of staff when appointed head – much enjoyment by small group of females.

> Patronising about family commitments. Women were worse than men.

It is heartening that many of the comments relating to the more overt forms of sexual harassment are in the past tense, but experiences of sexism were more likely to be reported by the younger than the older headteachers. Although the most blatant forms of the excluding masculine culture in the staffroom may be dying out, the underlying attitudes still seem evident.

Dealing with the stereotypes

The women heads deal with the negative stereotypes that impede their progress and working relationships with peers and subordinates mostly by trying to ignore them. Such avoidance has been discussed in respect of discrimination at the point of selection (see Chapter Three). When asked if they had experienced any sexism from those they worked with, about three quarters of the women heads in co-ed schools gave examples, particularly those that were married with children and the younger women. Yet about a quarter to a third of all the women respondents did not perceive any sexism.

The stereotypes considered in this chapter are generally negative and judgmental about the potential and the performance of women in leadership and management. However, the criticism claims that women are falling short of some 'male' standard of behaviour but that standard itself may not be the favoured style of management in schools (see Chapter Seven). The 'male' stereotypes reported are about a decisive, rational style of management that subdues any outward show of feelings or emotions. Underlying the generally negative stereotypes that sur-round women in headship is an implicit stereotype against which women (and men) are measured – of the leader who works harder, longer, is free from domestic constraints, produces quick and correct decisions and commands respect from staff and students so that there are no discipline problems. There are a number of important issues relating to the holding of this unthinking stereotype of leadership:

- This style of leadership is generally considered outmoded and in-adequate

- There are alternative styles of leadership that may be preferable in practice

- There is little opportunity for 'balance' in the implied mode of life of this idealised headteacher.

The tough stereotypical headteacher outlined above is increasingly less prevalent in schools. The harbouring of such inappropriate stereotypes by interviewers, peers, staff, parents and students in schools owes noth-ing to rationality. Much of what has been reported is backward looking.

> The stereotypes are now less overtly applied and the male cul-ture of the staffroom is diminishing. However, the evidence of the continuing application of the stereotypes against women can only be traced to the deep-rooted, patriarchal prejudices of society.

Conclusion

The present research on female secondary headteachers in England and Wales endorses the proposition in the literature that many secondary heads work in a predominantly masculine culture, which has the effect of marginalizing and isolating those women who do become heads and blocking the women who aspire to promotion and eventual headship. This culture mitigates against women taking leadership roles, or demands that they *prove* their worth as manager and leader.

Resentment by men of female leadership was the major theme to emerge from the headteachers' answers to questions about the sexism of peers and colleagues. This attitude is implicit in earlier research into masculine culture (Cunnison, 1989; Mac an Ghaill, 1994) but resentment of women in senior positions may not have been reported so clearly elsewhere. The responses indicated that men, and sometimes women, did not even feel the need to disguise their reluctance to have a woman leader, sometimes even threatening to resign.

These conclusions should be tempered however. Both men and women reveal a perception of gradual change and increased awareness, despite the fact that, in the words of one male head, ' Sexism is a fact of life – like attitudes to class, accent, race etc.[It is] to be confronted.'

Learning points for aspiring women:

- Recognise that there are entrenched social attitudes

- Remember that the stereotypical 'male' leader is an outdated notion

- Consider that there are alternative models of management and leadership

- Experience of running a home and motherhood can be relevant to leading a school.

Learning points for headteachers:

- Confront examples of sexism

- Examine the staffroom culture

- Think about the role model you offer

- Value alternative styles and experiences of management.

7
Exploding the myth of the masculine leader

- To be considered a good headteacher will I have to be seen to lead like a man?

What emerged from the prevailing stereotypes analysed in the last chapter was a negative stereotyping of women as falling short of a model of leadership identified with males. Research first undertaken in the 1970s and repeated in the 1990s by Schein (1994) was designed to test the underlying hypothesis that successful managers 'are perceived to possess those characteristics, attitudes and temperaments more commonly ascribed to men in general than to women in general' (p.41).

The research asks subjects which of the qualities listed they identify with men, with women and with successful middle managers. The outcomes have been consistent over time and across countries including the USA, UK, Germany, China and Japan. The results show a significant over-lapping between the qualities identified with men and those identified with successful management. Recently there has been a change in the ratings attributed by younger women, who are now starting to see women as more likely to have some of the traits necessary for successful management. The characteristics of the managerial (male) stereotype were:

leadership ability
ambitious
competitive
desires responsibility
skilled in business matters
competent
analytical ability.

Most women attributed similar ratings to men. Inclusion of management students in the research did not change the overall pattern, showing that younger male students, in particular, did not differ from their older counterparts in their views about the suitability women for management.

> The pervasiveness of managerial sex typing reflects the global devaluation of women. Embedded in all cultures are traditions, practices and views that impede women's social, political and economic equality. (Schein, 1994, p.51)

Some qualities that are identified with women, such as being supportive and involving others in decision-making processes, are now being recognised as valuable in a leader, although Gold (1996, p.422) makes the point that these skills could make women seem 'too 'soft' and ineffective to manage large organisations whilst the skills and attributes which were seen as important were linked to organisational efficiency and technical excellence'. These latter skills are generally identified as male characteristics.

> The behaviours, traits and characteristics displayed by men in formal positions of authority have become the 'givens' of leadership. Therefore, leadership in organizations has been historically associated with particular characteristics which are more frequently depicted as 'masculine' than 'feminine' — aggressiveness, forcefulness, competitiveness and independence. (Blackmore, 1989, p.100.)

Looking at management stereotypes from a masculine point of view, Collinson and Hearn (2000) identify the male operation of power, for example managers selecting men in their own image, inhabiting a formal bureaucratic structure and taking 'high risk' decisions. However, they also point to changes taking place in the gendered nature of management relations, noting the relative success of young women in junior management positions.

I have considered the masculine stereotype of leadership and the difficulties it causes women but there is also a positive stereotype of women that identifies them as nurturing, caring and people oriented (Noddings, 1992). At a time when emotional intelligence is being recognised as an essential component of leadership and management, this stereotype might even be thought to give women the advantage in terms of management style. The identification of transformational leadership as 'coming close to' the best approach to leadership for schools to meet today's challenges (Leithwood *et al*, 1999, p.21) appears to favour this stereotypical women's style, since transformational leadership is essentially based on relationships (Burns, 1978). One can now build a whole body of evidence and theory to establish a counter claim about leadership: that women are more suited for leadership than men.

Research has established that women tend to operate within a particular leadership style that involves collaboration, teamwork and empowerment. Summing up a range of studies, Blackmore (1994) states that:

> There is sufficient evidence in Australia, England, the USA, Canada and New Zealand to suggest that [the] top down model of change is not the preferred way of working of many female principals. (Blackmore 1994, p.18)

Studies in general management have also shown that: 'both female students and managers displayed a more participative leadership style', that 'they had a distinctive style of management which displayed more understanding and sympathy for others' and that women managers had a 'relations-oriented style' (studies quoted in Ferrario, 1994, pp.116-7).

However, such studies tend to treat women as a homogeneous group. Women and men cannot be regarded as two coherent groups that lead and manage in two distinctly different ways. Gold (1996) points out that 'profiles' of management style linked to men and women are unhelpful, since they make no allowance 'for any notion that some men manage sensitively and some women manage in a dominating and authoritarian fashion' (p.422).

A range of studies in general management shows that 'few actual gender differences in personal factors and behaviour have been consistently and empirically confirmed.' (Vinkenburg *et al*, 2000, p.130) The authors concede, however, that this may be because both sexes aspire to the accepted 'prototype' of manager and that the evaluation of women as managers is biased by social expectations that can cause identical behaviour by men and women managers to be judged differently. In education, research undertaken by Evetts (1994) with ten female and ten male heads led to the conclusion that leadership and management behaviour were not necessarily gender based:

Some of the male heads emphasized collegial relations and participatory forms of management in schools while some of the female heads were inclined towards hierarchy and authority in management. Significant differences in styles of leadership are not difficult to demonstrate in general ... although the clear linkage of style with gender is more problematic. (Evetts, 1994, p.88)

However, Evetts (1994) agrees that: 'it is not difficult to show gender differences in the *experience* of headship' (p.89 original emphasis.) Although a range of styles may be expected from both men and women, there is agreement that the perceptions of the ways in which men and women operate may be differentiated and that the social experience of being a leader is different for men and women.

'Masculine' and 'feminine' as ideal types

There is an overlap in the behaviour of men and women leaders. There is a spectrum of management behaviour that includes 'masculine' and 'feminine', and within this range, it tends to be presumed that 'feminine' behaviour is more associated with women than with men. Research undertaken by Bem (1974) developed a Sex-Role Inventory, which identifies ideal types of masculine and feminine behaviour.

Table 7.1 Bem Sex Role Inventory

Masculine	Feminine
acts as leader	affectionate
aggressive	cheerful
ambitious	childlike
analytical	compassionate
assertive	does not use harsh language
athletic	eager to soothe hurt feelings
competitive	feminine
defends own beliefs	flattering
dominant	gentle
forceful	gullible
has leadership abilities	loves children
independent	loyal
individualistic	sensitive to the needs of others
makes decisions easily	shy
masculine	soft spoken
self-reliant	sympathetic
self-sufficient	tender
strong personality	understanding
willing to take a stand	warm
willing to take risks	yielding
(Bem. 1974, p.157)	

Subjects were then asked to grade themselves and could thus be given a score for masculinity and femininity – and androgyny. The identification of these attributes is not intended to label males and females. The recognition of the importance of environmental factors means that in social psychological terms:

> Females and males can be brought up with the capacity to express a range of characteristics independently, whether they have traditionally been viewed as 'masculine' or 'feminine'. For instance, men can be tender and women assertive. (Nelson-Jones, 1986, p.44)

The concept of psychological androgyny envisages that a range of qualities drawn from both lists can be found in managers. In later work, Bem (1977) stated that for individuals scoring high on both masculine and feminine characteristics:

> The concept of psychological androgyny implies that it is possible for an individual to be both assertive and compassionate, both instrumental and expressive, both masculine and feminine, depending upon the situational appropriateness of these various modalities; and it further implies that an individual may even blend these complementary modalities in a single act, being able, for example, to fire an employee if the circumstances warrant it but with sensitivity for the human emotion that such an act inevitably produces. (p.196)

Those rated as androgynous, i.e. scoring highly on both masculine and feminine ratings, showed greater independence, ability to nurture and self-esteem than those who scored low on both. Ferrario (1994, p.116) reports that such 'androgynous' individuals: 'are able to respond more effectively than either masculine or feminine individuals to a wide variety of situations'.

A similar range of masculine and feminine qualities has been used by Gray (1993) in his work on training female and male headteachers. The qualities are presented as gender paradigms, and are used to open up discussion about gender and issues such as self-awareness. The gender paradigms themselves, like those of Bem (1974), could be seen to represent the dualism of rationality versus emotionalism that subtly renders the female as of inferior status or, alternatively, that could be used to reduce gender differences to essentialist labelling.

Table 7.2 Gender Paradigms (Gray, 1993)

The nurturing/feminine paradigm	The defensive/aggressive masculine paradigm
caring	highly regulated
creative	conformist
intuitive	normative
aware of individual differences	competitive
non-competitive	evaluative
tolerant	disciplined
subjective	objective
informal.	formal.

(Gray, 1993, p.111)

Gray does not intend to label the sexes and recognises that generalisations that rigidly differentiate male and female management styles are inappropriate. Interestingly, he does comment on differential reactions to these paradigms, which indicate the relative sensitivities and the importance to men and women of gender issues:

> If I use these paradigms with large mixed groups of teachers, I invariably get very positive reactions from women, leading to excited discussion, but from men I receive not so much a negative response as an indifferent one. It therefore seems to me that women are much more aware of gender issues at a quite complex level, but that men are nonplussed when these issues are raised. (Gray, 1993, p.112)

This reaction to the introduction of gender issues was also found in the survey of women and men headteachers undertaken for this book. The women were expansive and wrote extensive comments. Many seemed genuinely delighted to be asked questions that related to gender and management. The response rate of the men was only nine per cent less than that of the women (61 per cent against 70 per cent) but they wrote far less than the women, with a very few exceptions, and there was genuine puzzlement about some of the questions that related gender to management, for example the question on 'proving your worth as a male manager'. Similarly, the questions about sexism were generally related to women and only rarely to the possibility of sexist stereotyping of men (see Chapter Six).

I used the gender paradigms of Gray (1993) in the interviews (Coleman, 1996b) and the two surveys. In both cases the headteachers were asked to indicate which of the qualities they felt applied to them, without any linking of the qualities to gender.

How the headteachers perceived themselves in terms of gender paradigms

Table 7.3 Qualities identified from male and female paradigms of Gray (1993)
% indicating that they felt they had the quality

Female paradigm	women	men
Aware of individual differences	86.0	84.0
Caring	79.4	84.2
Intuitive	76.2	66.0
Tolerant	68.7	79.6
Creative	63.0	54.1
Informal	59.4	60.4
Non-competitive	21.5	17.0
Subjective	13.8	13.3
Male paradigm		
Evaluative	61.1	70.0
Disciplined	60.4	51.0
Competitive	50.6	57.3
Objective	50.6	61.7
Formal	14.9	18.2
Highly regulated	13.2	11.4
Conformist	10.9	13.6
Normative	4.0	7.0

The outcomes show conclusively that the paradigms are not perceived as relevant in distinguishing women from men. There are great similarities between the adjectives chosen most often by men and women headteachers. From the female paradigm, the women are slightly more likely to choose 'aware of individual differences' and 'non-competitive', 'intuitive' and 'creative'. The men are more likely to choose 'caring' and 'tolerant', ironically, two adjectives that are very much identified with the concept of the ethic of care in the idealised woman leader. In the male paradigm, in every case except 'disciplined', the men were more likely than the women to identify themselves as having these 'male' qualities. Therefore there appears to be greater convergence by both men and women towards the feminine paradigm, although some elements of the male paradigm still hold a little stronger for the men. Both sets of adjectives are androgynous, in the sense that the headteachers see themselves as drawing on a wide range of attributes deemed both 'feminine' and 'masculine'.

By looking at the qualities most and least identified, another table of the self perceptions of female and male headteachers emerges.

Table 7.4 Qualities identified by 50 per cent or more of the women headteachers

		%
Aware of individual differences	(f)	86.0
Caring	(f)	79.4
Intuitive	(f)	76.2
Tolerant	(f)	68.7
Creative	(f)	63.0
Evaluative	(m)	61.1
Disciplined	(m)	60.4
Informal	(f)	59.4
Competitive	(m)	50.6
Objective	(m)	50.6
(f) = feminine	(m) = masculine	

Table 7.5 Qualities identified by 50 per cent or more of the men headteachers

Caring	84.2	(f)
Aware of individual differences	84.0	(f)
Tolerant	79.6	(f)
Evaluative	70.0	(m)
Intuitive	66.0	(f)
Objective	61.7	(m)
Informal	60.4	(f)
Competitive	57.3	(m)
Creative	54.1	(f)
Disciplined	51.0	(m)
(f) = feminine	(m) = masculine	

The qualities identified by over 50 per cent of the men and women are the same, with the relatively small differences already identified above. Even where the difference between women and men is in the region of ten per cent, as with 'tolerant' identified by 68.7 per cent of the women and 79.6 per cent of the men, this may be tempered by another concept, e.g. 'aware of individual differences' identified by 86.0 per cent of the women and just slightly less of the men. It is interesting that three of the five female headteachers interviewed (Coleman, 1996b, p.167) tended to be ambivalent about tolerance:

> I am tolerant in a lot of things but I don't suffer fools.

> Tolerant only to a degree, I have to say. If somebody is being downright awkward, bloody-minded or not willing to see the light, I'm not prepared to put up with that.

> Sometimes I'm intolerant, can't stand low standards and sloppiness and idleness and so I am a bit intolerant.

Other noteworthy differences in the survey emerge for the words 'intuitive', 'evaluative' and 'disciplined', each of which were chosen by around ten per cent more women than men. Intuitive is a 'feminine' concept whereas the others are 'masculine'.

Table 7.6 Qualities identified by less than 20 per cent of the men headteachers

	%	
Formal	18.2	(m)
Non-competitive	17.0	(f)
Conformist	13.6	(m)
Subjective	13.3	(f)
Highly regulated	11.4	(m)
Normative	7.0	(m)

Table 7.7 Qualities identified by less than 20 per cent of the women headteachers

		%	
Formal	(m)	14.9	(m)
Subjective	(f)	13.8	(f)
Highly regulated	(m)	13.2	(m)
Conformist	(m)	10.9	(m)
Normative	(m)	4.0	(m)
(f) = feminine (m) = masculine			

Non-competitive is the only adjective that appears in one list and not the other. It was still identified by similar proportions of men and women. Only 20 per cent of the women headteachers and 17 percent of the men picked it.

> Therefore there appears to be very little difference in the qualities that are both most often and least often identified by women and men in terms of how they perceive their management style.

Although most of the women chose mostly feminine traits, quite a few masculine ones were also listed. Interestingly, most of the men picked predominantly feminine traits. Clearly the self-perception of most of them does not conform to the traditional male conceptualisations of leadership and management

The findings of the in-depth interviews with female headteachers were validated by the survey data. All five headteachers identified themselves as being caring, creative, intuitive and aware of individual differences. From the 'masculine' list, the headteachers saw themselves as evaluative, disciplined and objective. Gray considers the 'masculine' paradigm as 'a defence against self-awareness (Gray, 1993, p.112) but the headteachers equated the three 'masculine' adjectives they chose with fairness rather than coldness:

> Evaluative, if in the sense of making sure that we are evaluating what we're doing, testing it out on people for their attitude and their opinion – yes. Discipline, I suppose ... if what it means is giving people the opportunity to be involved, not just having a free-for-all where somebody might be ignored. But certainly not with any kind of authoritarian stamp on it. (female headteacher quoted in Coleman, 1996b, p.166)

In the masculine paradigm identified by Gray (1993), the term 'objective' is a denial of emotion. But the headteachers saw objectivity as preferable to subjectivity, and objectivity as a state that they strove to attain. Seeking objectivity was linked with a view that management

> ...has to be enlightened and aware and compassionate. I don't mean soft, I mean that we're going to be making demands on people for all sorts of standards, for training and outcomes and everything, we've got to do our

very best to ensure that we recognise what people are doing and that we enable them to do it as well as we possibly can. (female headteacher, in Coleman 1996, p.167)

A collaborative style of management

The collaborative and participative style of management encouraging the empowerment of others, and with an emphasis on working in teams, is the style most strongly identified with women leaders. Reference is only occasionally made to other styles among women leaders (see Evetts, 1994). The value that women may bring to management has been recognised in trans-national corporations, who see: 'women managers as bringing needed collaborative and participative skills to the workplace' (Adler, 1994, p.26).

For the female headteachers in Hall's study, 'the women heads' preference for working collaboratively was manifest in their support for teamwork, particularly when working with senior colleagues' (Hall, 1996, p.189).

The interviewed headteachers (Coleman, 1996b) all acknowledged the importance of collaboration and consultation, but stopped short of pure democracy:

> It has to be consultative. Very early in my headship here I announced to staff that I was going to create an open management style and I think they misinterpreted that everybody would be deciding things and I would just be sitting back and listening and letting it all happen. So we had to correct that one fairly early on.

> It's consultative and participatory as much as possible. Having said that, it's not democratic in the sense of ... having staff room votes on issues, so it's consultative through a framework of a consultation structure, but at the end of the day I think decisions are made by the management team, having consulted and that's it.

> (female heads quoted in Coleman, 1996b, p.169)

The desire to create an open and consultative climate was linked both with the belief that it would increase efficiency and with the concern for people that was evident in their choice of adjectives from the gender paradigms:

> I honestly feel so much more comfortable when things are open because I think you can tackle problems better, you can have far better solutions to everything that is going on anyway and you're just using peoples' strengths all the time. I think it creates a much better working relationship with people. (*ibid.*)

Quantitative research undertaken in the UK by Jirasinghe and Lyons (1996) gives further support to the identification of a collaborative style of management predominating amongst female headteachers. In a large scale study of male and female primary and secondary heads, Jirasinghe and Lyons administered a variety of well-tried personality tests, including the Occupational Personality Questionnaire (OPQ), the Belbin Team Types questionnaire, and a leadership styles questionnaire derived from the work of Bass (1981).

The most striking finding of the leadership styles questionnaire was that the women tended to identify themselves as participative and consultative leaders whereas the male heads identified themselves as delegative leaders. Although there is not a great deal of difference between participative and delegative leaders, there were differences in the way the female and male heads perceived themselves:

> Female heads claim a preference for a style of leadership, which favours consensus decision making; seeking the involvement of all relevant colleagues thereby securing their commitment and motivation; and a warm and friendly social style. (Jirasinghe and Lyons, 1996, p.61)

Whereas the male delegative leadership style meant that:

> They tend to communicate less with their staff and are inclined not to give clearly defined instructions or plan the work of the personnel they oversee. Such leaders tend not to seek the staffs' views as to how projects should be conducted, but are inclined simply to hand over the work to be done. (*ibid.* p.61)

The findings of Jirasinghe and Lyons also included an element of directiveness in the styles of all the headteachers, something that differentiated them from managers outside education. Hall (1996) makes a similar observation in summing up the management and leadership style of the six female heads in her study. She notes that they had a clear view of their own role in the school as the key person, with a vision for the school:

A picture emerges of women heads enacting strong leadership within a collaborative framework. ... [They] were firmly committed to the belief that sharing leadership still required them to take the lead when appropriate, including having a personal vision for the school. (Hall, 1996, p.190).

The identification of women with collaborative management styles is therefore subject to modification. Firstly, although they may consult and collaborate, they tend to take the final decisions themselves with their management team. Secondly, as Jirasinghe and Lyons (1996) found, male and female headteachers may be more alike in style than managers outside education. In particular, both sexes may be fairly directive while maintaining a consultative mode. Reay and Ball (2000, p.151) point out that there is no essentialist: 'playing out of fixed gender behaviour' when women take on leadership roles but that: 'new evolving gender identities which transgress normative gender divisions' (*ibid*) may emerge.

The outcomes of the survey seem to confirm the preference for collaboration on the part of women, but they also indicate that this style is favoured by male headteachers. This chimes with the similarity of style between men and women heads identified by Jirasinghe and Lyons (1996). The fact that the management styles are self-reported in the survey makes it difficult to discriminate between actual collaboration versus delegation – the subtle difference they found.

Key words to describe the headteachers' style of management

When faced with a pre-determined list, choices are constrained and views may be influenced. To avoid this the headteachers were asked to list three words that they believed best described their style of management before seeing the adjectives in the masculine/feminine paradigms. No guidance was given, so allowing unprompted responses. A remarkably large range of adjectives was offered. It was possible to group them, however, to establish the styles of management that the headteachers thought that they adopted.

As with the adjectives cited in the paradigms, the differences in the perceptions of the women and men about their management styles were slight. I originally analysed the women's adjectives and identified the themes that emerged. The same themes worked with the men; the proportion who chose similar words was virtually the same. It seems that in terms of their perceptions of what they hope and think they are doing, women and men headteachers think along similar lines.

When all the adjectives together were analysed for each sex, the following grouping emerged. The adjectives quoted as examples of each style were those most often stated in the category:

1. A collaborative style of management; e.g. consultative, open, participative

2. A people-oriented style of management; e.g. team related, supportive, caring.

3. An autocratic/directive style of management: e.g. decisive, firm, strong.

4. An efficient style of management; e.g. energetic, focused, hands on, planning.

5. A values style of management; e.g. visionary, fair, honest, trusting.

Table 7.8 Styles of management identified by adjectives chosen

	Women		Men	
	No. of words	% of total	No. of words	% of total
Collaborative	458	38.5	401	40.0
People-oriented	283	23.8	212	21.3
Autocratic/directive	177	14.9	119	11.9
Efficient	139	11.6	126	12.7
Values	132	11.1	138	13.9

The women tend to be more likely than the men to choose words relating to people, and, paradoxically, also are more likely to choose words like 'autocratic'. For example, it was a woman head who styled herself: 'bloody-minded, belligerent and aggressive'. The men are slightly more likely to choose words that are related to collaboration, efficiency and values. However, the single most popular terms to indicate a style of management used by both sexes matched my term 'collaborative'. The potentially overlapping 'people-oriented' style of management was also strongly indicated by the adjectives chosen. These two broad categories suggest a favoured style of management for both men and women that is consistent with the adjectives most often chosen from the feminine paradigm: 'aware of individual differences', 'caring', 'intuitive' and 'tolerant'. The majority of adjectives fell within these two categories and 'open, supportive and encouraging' (female headteacher) was a typical entry crossing both categories.

When choosing their adjectives, the headteachers seemed well aware that a more collegial style of management is now generally rated as normatively superior (Wallace, 1989; Bush 1995). Heads do appear to realise that they should try to move towards such a style (Hustler *et al*, 1995). However, the majority of the survey heads stopped short of collegiality and preferred terms like collaborative and participatory to describe their management style.

In a study of managers in general (Charlesworth, 1997) the respondents to a questionnaire were asked to choose from eleven adjectives the ones that described their own management style. Her findings were quite similar to mine, the most popular adjective being participative, chosen by over 60 per cent of the women and 50 per cent of the men.

Although fewer heads opted for the adjectives I called either 'autocratic/ directive' or 'efficient' a substantial number identified at least some aspects of their management style as closer to the rational, efficient male paradigm than the caring nurturing female one. It tallied with some of the 'masculine' adjectives from the Gray list, such as 'disciplined', 'evaluative', 'formal' and 'competitive'.

The final group of adjectives represents a strand of thinking that, though not contradicting the others identifies values that may well underpin the management style of many headteachers. The category of 'management driven by values' is not stereotypically male or female. No headteacher listed all three adjectives in this category but many combined them with adjectives classified elsewhere, for example: 'collaborative, consistent and fair' – fair being classified as a 'values' adjective. I noted that the heads of religious schools were no more likely than the others to have listed 'values' adjectives.

After considering all the adjectives together, I looked at the groups of three. Where at least two were consistent in coming from one group, that was the dominant style I attributed to the individual. For example, I place the male headteacher who listed himself as 'decisive, innovative, fair,' in the 'efficient' category, another who chose: 'open, fair, consultative' in the 'collaborative' category. The groups of three adjectives were most likely to come from one of two major groupings: either collaborative and/or people oriented on the one side, and on the other, from either the autocratic and/or efficient types, with the majority overall coming from the collaborative/people oriented side of the spectrum. If we look at a binary division of collaborative/people oriented versus efficient/autocratic, most of the adjective groups are internally inconsistent but there are a few which are not. For example, one woman describes herself as consultative, considerate (occasionally) and autocratic, and one man stated that he was: 'a mixture of autocratic and empowering therefore 'intensely irritating''. Obviously nothing short of a full case study would allow full analysis of these responses!

Overall, there appears to be a range of management styles indicated with the large majority of the headteachers adopting a 'collaborative' and/or 'people-orientated' style of management on one side of the spectrum and a minority operating an autocratic/directive style characterised by 'efficient' adjectives on the other. The 'values driven' style tends to underpin the remaining styles (see Figure 7.1).

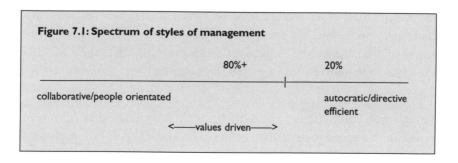

Figure 7.1: Spectrum of styles of management

80%+   20%

collaborative/people orientated   autocratic/directive efficient

<———values driven———>

Age and management style

It appears that at least 80 per cent of the headteachers see themselves as having a collaborative/people-orientated style. However, the autocratic/ directive and/or efficient style is adopted by a minority – slightly more women than men and more of these women aged 50 or over. This style is more easily identified with the 'masculine' stereotype of management which focuses on direction, targets and efficiency rather than collaboration, empowerment and caring. Reay and Ball (2000) argue that the increasing marketisation of education is likely to influence heads to operate in 'masculine' ways.

The age differential in the women was statistically significant but age was not a differentiating factor among the men. The group of women over 50 are significantly more likely to operate in an autocratic and directive manner than any other group of headteachers, but they are a tiny minority overall.

> There is little difference overall between the men and women in terms of their perceptions of their management style, but there is a distinct difference between the perceptions of the younger and older women.

There has been speculation that younger headteachers might be more collaborative in their management style. In comparing 'old' with newly appointed headteachers, Weindling and Earley (1987) commented:

> The cohort of new heads saw themselves as being more consultative and open to the views of staff than their predecessors were, and they felt their style of headship involved an 'open door' approach towards staff, pupils and parents. (p.181)

Several heads in the study undertaken by Hustler *et al* (1995) comment on a change in their management style over the years, towards being more consultative and supportive. One man, Christopher Hampson, specifically stated that his management style had altered dramatically.

> Perhaps I was something of a benevolent despot or even an autocrat ... had to really because there was not any structure for decision-making in a context of necessary change. Now I operate much more of a collegiate senior management system. (Hustler, *et al* 1995, p.49)

The older women in the survey appear to have become less collaborative and more directive with age, or to have inherited a type of behaviour at the time when a 'male' style of management was expected of them. That this style is more prevalent amongst the older women probably indicates that their ways of operating owe more to their past experience than to the current experience of marketisation with its implications for rational, efficient, 'male' management, which might be expected to have affected all headteachers equally.

Teamwork

Teamwork, combined with a collaborative style of working, appears to be the favoured management style of female headteachers. Grace (1995) emphasises the importance to women of teamwork, which they regard as a natural way of working rather than an imposition. The head-teachers in Hall's (1996) study also exhibited a preference for working in teams. Experience in general management confirms that women tend to work well and naturally in teams (Davidson and Cooper, 1992, Cartwright and Gale (1995) whereas men may regard it with suspicion (David, 1988).

When the female headteachers chose their own words for their management style, they mentioned team-related terms more than the men, associating them with people management and collaborative working terms as the preferred management style of most heads. The heads I interviewed all stressed the importance of teams in their schools, and all had promoted teamwork and considered teams an important aspect of school management:

> Most things we would try to do in teams. ... People tend to work in little groups because then you can share the responsibility of it (female head-teacher, quoted in Coleman, 1996b, p.171)

Empowerment of those in the teams is essential, so empowerment follows naturally from collaboration and teamwork. The success of female heads in empowering others has been established in headteacher research in Britain (Jones, 1987; Hall, 1996) and the USA (Gross and Trask, 1976; Shakeshaft, 1989; Grogan, 1996). My research endorsed this finding, with empowerment being mentioned by heads, along with adjectives that implied concern for staff, and a participatory, collaborative approach. Three times as many women as men used words specifically relating to teams. Reay and Ball (2000) point out the value of teams for all heads:

> While many staff perceive them as participative and empowering, for the headteacher they are also about gaining broader support for an initiative and assistance in getting it developed.' (p.152)

Although this may be true, some of the studies mentioned above (Hall, 1996, Shakeshaft, 1989) suggest that team work seems more typical of women.

Validating the self-perception of headteachers
The data gathered from the surveys and interviews was not triangulated within the schools. No other members of staff were asked how they perceived the management and leadership style of the headteacher. Qualitative studies such as Hall's (1996) give a more rounded perception of the style of the headteachers. In relation to people and teamwork she concludes that:

> Observations of their interactions with senior colleagues and governors supported the claims they made about their preferred uses of power to promote teamwork rather than to dominate. (p.182)

A quantitative study undertaken with 194 schools in Hong Kong involved triangulation of the perception of the headteacher with the views of the teachers. Here the teachers appeared more critical of the principals than they were of themselves. However, the discrepancies between the perceptions of the teachers and the self-perceptions of the headteachers were smaller for the women heads and larger for the men. In other words, the women's perceptions seemed to be more accurate (Kingman, 1996, pp.352-3). This difference in perception may be linked to the probability of men being more confident than women and more likely to overstate their abilities (Shakeshaft, 1989; Al Khalifa, 1992; Davies and Gunawardena, 1993; Still, 1995).

Although the present survey of heads was not triangulated by the views of others in the schools, they were asked about the ways in which they operate.

Accessibility
I asked the headteachers a few questions about their style of management particularly about their availability to staff, and the amount of time they spent out of the office when in school. Most, both men and women, claimed to make themselves available to their staff whenever possible (see Table 7.9).

Table 7.9: Opportunities for staff to talk to the head

	women %	men %
Any time if not in meeting	84.3	87.6
Any time within specified limits	8.9	9.2
By appointment	6.8	2.0

Although all showed a perhaps surprising willingness to make themselves available, it was generally the younger men who were slightly less willing to see people at any time.

Time spent out of the office

The headteachers also appear to be around in the school for a considerable amount of their time (see Table 7.10). In answer to the question: 'while you are in school, what proportion of your time do you spend out of your office?' approximately 80 per cent spent between ten per cent and 50 per cent of their time in the school but out of their office, with more men than women spending up to 75 per cent of their time in this way.

Table 7.10: Time spent out of office

% of time	women %	men %
under 10%	3.5	2.0
10% – 25%	32.0	25.2
25% – 50%	47.9	48.4
50% – 75%	16.6	24.4

They were not asked how the time was spent, but presumably some of it would be in teaching and some would involve 'management by walking about'. This plus the availability of most of them to teachers suggests a dominant management style in line with the one most headteachers reported. It seems that most operate in an open way and are closely involved with their staff and the operation of the school. Findings from the USA (Shakeshaft, 1989) showed that women spend more time than men interacting with both staff and students. The evidence here indicates that in the UK high levels of interaction are equally true for women and men. Given the current emphasis on the monitoring of achievement this is hardly surprising.

Conclusion

This chapter has focused on the ways in which gender relates to management and leadership. There is a basic and pervasive stereotype which identifies management and leadership with maleness and this underlies both theories and practice. Cultural feminism has identified that the archetypal view of women as caring and nurturing may mean that women naturally offer a superior style of management and leadership, but this in turn re-emphasises the dualism that can establish men as superior.

> Presenting women as a homogeneous category recycles the modernist storyline that women, because of their differences, even in leadership, merely complement men. (Blackmore, 1999, p.58)

In addition, it cannot be true that all women manage in a certain way and all men in another.

The identification of women with a collaborative style of management in terms of their own perceptions is generally borne out by the survey findings. However, the survey of male heads shows that most of them also perceive themselves as collaborative and caring managers. The 'masculine' style of management, a rational model that stresses efficiency, outcomes and target setting, does not appear to be the style most favoured. In fact, the largest single group appearing to operate thus is 20 per cent or so of the women headteachers aged 50 or over.

Although the preferred mode of leadership of both men and women is collaborative and people-centred, all the headteachers are operating within a culture that is generally slanted to men's advantage. Whatever the relevance of masculine and feminine management styles to male and female leaders, the experience of women headteachers is likely to be contextualised by their gender.

> There is no ungendered experience, only experiences of men and women of different sexuality, race and ethnicity. Ultimately such dualisms maintain unequal power relations. (Blackmore, 1995, p.53)

The influences of assumptions concerning gender are pervasive and are likely to affect the leadership role and style of management adopted by every educational manager. In her study of female heads, Hall (1996) contextualises the gender differentiated experience of the current cohort of headteachers in England and Wales. In her study she assumes

> ...commonalities in women's experiences of leading schools in Britain which could be attributed to at least two factors: their socialization as girls and women in post-war Britain and the gendered nature of organizations (for example, women's lower pay, unequal promotion opportunities, prevalence of sexual harassment). (p.3)

My findings show that the female and male leaders do not perceive themselves as operating in distinctively different ways and that the ideal types of gender do not necessarily differentiate how men and women manage. The findings of Jirasinghe and Lyons based on validated psychometric tests are similar to those of my survey but make an important distinction between the prevalent participative style of women and the delegative style of men. However, what is reported in my survey is self-perception, and is mainly based on the compilation of answers to a postal questionnaire. Qualitative studies, for example that of Hall (1996), bring depth of observation and long scrutiny. Studies of male and female communication (Schick-Case, 1994) show consistent differences in male and female speech which must surely affect the ways they manage and are perceived to manage. Certainly, as the previous chapter showed, the ways in which women and men experience being the headteachers of their schools are different. In the end, the men are seen as being in the 'correct' place and the women are challenging the norm. Women bring to their work experiences of life of a different kind to those of men.

'Will I have to be seen to lead like a man if I am going to be considered a good headteacher?' The answer is both yes and no. Certainly the experiences of some of the older women headteachers has led them to believe that they should operate according to a male mode of management. However, the majority of headteachers of both sexes actually perceive themselves as leading in a 'feminine' style, and the normatively acceptable ways of operating advocated in the current literature on leadership also favours such a style of management.

Learning points for aspiring women:

- The majority of heads see themselves as operating in a way that could be termed 'feminine'

- Most heads of both sexes favours the collaborative and people-orientated styles

- This perception by the headteachers remains in a context where the identification of leadership is with men.

Learning points for headteachers:

- Most headteachers, whether male or female, see themselves as collaborative and people orientated

- Nonetheless differences remain in the ways those women and men experience their headship.

8

Being a woman headteacher: constraints, problems and liberation

- What is it like to be a woman headteacher?

- How can I make it to the top? What can be learned from the experience of today's headteachers?

Most women headteachers will feel exposed and isolated at times. This will obviously depend partly on their own psychological profile but also on where their schools are situated and whether they are girls' schools, co-educational or (very rarely) boys' schools. Most women headteachers are found in London and to a lesser extent in other major conurbations (see Chapter One). A similar pattern probably applies elsewhere certainly, I was aware when in China and South Africa that women principals might be found in the cities but not in rural areas.

About a third of the women headteachers in England and Wales head girls' schools and they were slightly less likely to report sexist attitudes than those in the co-ed schools. However, many of them have worked in mixed schools and all attend meetings of headteachers with their mainly male peers. Such meetings have been reported as potentially stressful (see Chapter Six).

Considering what is it like to be a woman leader more broadly, the evidence from official statistics in the UK and elsewhere is that women are under-represented in leadership and management positions in education as in other arenas. The reasons are complex, the consequence of cultural and social assumptions about the division of sex roles. The stereotypical attitudes support men in achievement in the public domain and locate women in a supporting role, derived from an atavistic identification of women with the private domain of domesticity and motherhood. As a result women who do become leaders in education are likely to feel a discontinuity. As Reay and Ball (2000, p.147) put it: 'there remains an inherent paradox in women occupying the upper echelons of any public sector profession because such a positioning confounds and contradicts traditional notions of femininity'.

As can be seen by the responses of the women headteachers in my survey, the majority perceived sexism both when they were given the job and while they were doing it, when many experienced feelings of isolation. Such experiences and perceptions are likely to affect many of the interpersonal dealings of the headteachers. The underlying approval given to a male holding a position of power means that gender is simply not an issue for men, although they may recognise that it is for women. There are some exceptions to this particularly in the case of men who do not match common preconceptions and stereotypes about maleness. For the women, gender is likely to create tensions in particular areas of their work, for example when dealing with male resentment of their leadership or countering expectations of governors about how they will handle discipline problems.

The impact of career on family and choices about having children has been considered in Chapters Four and Five. However, it bears repeating that since women tend to take much of the responsibility for children, the decision to have a child and whether to have more than one is particularly difficult for a woman who aspires to a leadership job. The demands of being a headteacher were reported by both men and women in the survey. Men talked about how their job impacted on their wives and children, but many handed major responsibility for family life to their wives, whereas it is relatively rare for husbands or male partners to take this role. 94 per cent of the men headteachers have a child or children, compared to just over 50 per cent of the women, and even less among those under 50. Women are therefore compelled to decide whether to put their career first, defer their career or try to combine senior professional responsibilities with motherhood. It may be that life choices for both men and women will be weighed and balanced differently by the next generation of managers and leaders, but in a society that still puts so much value on paid work and career advancement change is likely to be slow.

The subjects of this book are the women and men headteachers who have already taken their major life decisions about career and family. This chapter considers how gender influences the ways in which they perceive themselves as headteachers. A headteacher is in a prominent and generally respected role, whether directly with staff and pupils, or with parents, governors or headteacher colleagues and others external to the school such as the local education authority and local businesses. Important to playing that role is their own self-concept and their perceptions of how others perceive them. I was particularly interested in how their gender impinged on this and asked the women if, as a headteacher, they had ever found it an advantage to be a woman. In the second survey of the men, I asked them whether they had ever found it advantageous to be a man.

The effect of gender on the role of headteacher

The last chapter concluded that although men and women seem to perceive themselves as managing in similar ways, their experiences as headteachers differ. The women's experience apparently enabled them to see the effect of gender on their role in a way that they men did not.

Although only a minority of men commented on gender as an issue, I consider their responses before exploring the varied responses of the women. It is difficult to avoid the conclusion that gender is not often an issue for men in a society where they are still seen as the natural leaders.

Male responses

Only about a quarter of the men in the survey commented on the relevance of gender to their becoming and being a headteachers, whereas two thirds of the women recognised its importance and often observed that their gender could be an advantage to them as a women head (more of this later).

Men as leaders

The naturalness of being a headteacher for the men meant that they did not remark on the fact that as a man they had 'made it'. It may be difficult for men to recognise that society favours them for leadership roles and faced with a direct question about this, only 22.7 per cent of them said that 'men are generally preferred in management'.

> People tell me they prefer working for a man!
>
> The very conservative rural community expected it 15 years ago.
>
> No examples, but a strong opinion that I have been challenged less as a result of being male.
>
> (male heads)

Sometimes this recognition was faint:

> There remains some suggestion of exclusivity in some areas – or is it my imagination?

Dealing with parents and pupils

Some of the men saw definite advantage in terms of dealing with aggressive parents and difficult pupils, yet the women felt that they had the advantage, too, (see below). However, the men considered that they were helped by their physical appearance and that:

> Working class parents will accept things from me that would cause a woman more problems.
>
> I believe being male is an expectation of some parents as a 'tough' school and area.

The recognition of a preference for male leaders was attributed particularly to the Muslim community:

> Most of our parents are Asian, with traditional outlooks. Many fathers prefer to deal with a man. However, I constantly seek ways of getting women colleagues to take a full share of working with such parents – i.e. it is important to change some parental perspectives and stereotypes.

Benefits of having a wife

The job of being a headteacher is difficult and demanding. As a man, the benefits of having a supportive wife were particularly recognised by some:

> Within my marriage arrangement the 'man' has the public career. I could not do what I do without my wife. In a real sense it takes two people (seven if you include my children) to do my job. All of us have made great sacrifices. Time will tell whether we have been wise.

Backlash against feminist ideas

Although most of the men did not feel that their gender had any relevance to their position as headteachers, a small number did make reference to the 'backlash' phenomenon (Lingard and Douglas, 1999), perceiving sexist stereotyping as directed at them and generating disadvantages in being male:

> Regrettably, I sense there is/was an advantage. Less so now; possibly the opposite, as we are now the group damaged by sexist stereotyping.

> I felt it more difficult as a man to achieve deputy headship.

There is a perception that schools seek a gender balance for deputy heads so schools might be seeking women at this level. In reality, 36 per cent of all secondary deputy heads in England and Wales are women (DfEE, 2000a), far more than women heads but certainly not indicating that women are favoured.

Stereotypical male behaviour

The following comment is one of the very few from the whole survey to address the issues of stereotypical male leadership behaviour from the point of view of a man who recognises it and does not approve. Even though the majority of both men and women believe that they are managing in a collaborative/nurturing 'feminine' way there is a great deal of evidence from the women that 'masculine' ways of behaving still dominate, particularly in gatherings of headteachers, local government and governors. One male headteacher responded to the question about being a man:

> There are disadvantages as well [of being a man], e.g. being expected to be part of the 'men's club' and spending time talking to those boring men. I don't.

There were also limited examples of other men who had rejected what they saw as a stereotypical male management style and overtly adopted a very different and more 'feminine' style, which sometimes led to difficulties:

> It may have been a disadvantage to arrive as head in a very 'male/macho' school and try to change the ethos.

> I used very particular 'female' traits to improve relationships at the school and engender trust and respect. I followed a very 'male' headteacher!

These comments indicate a sophisticated awareness of gender issues as they apply to management and they echo the call of Collinson and Hearn (1996; 2000) and others for a re-assessment of men in management and for the concept of a masculine style to be replaced by one of 'masculinities'.

Female responses

The main advantages identified by the women, were linked to the surprise for others of finding a woman leader in a position normally perceived as automatically male. What comes through is their relish in being a headteacher and having the status and power to operate as they wish. These women – still a minority – occupy relatively powerful positions and appreciate the strength and opportunities this gives them. The surprise element and the status combine in situations where men might be expected to take an aggressive stance.

Defusing 'macho' behaviour

The largest proportion of comments from the women about how their gender impacted on being a headteacher related to the ability to defuse aggressive male behaviour, particularly by fathers and adolescent boys but also sometimes male staff:

> Men (staff or parents) are less aggressive – they don't have to maintain their 'macho' image with me.

> Angry teenage boys are not threatened by a woman – reason can prevail before the discipline.

> Avoidance of confrontation. Ability to be myself rather than play the role of 'headmaster'. I'm glad to be a woman in this job.

The women appear to make use of their 'difference'. This advantage is contrary to that expected by more traditional governors, who doubted whether women headteachers would be able to handle discipline problems, particularly with teenage boys. The women link this ability to their management style:

> A woman can defuse conflict more easily, perhaps 'soft' management styles can work if used judiciously.

The unusual aspect of being a woman in a male role can definitely be an advantage, particularly outside the school. The local education authority or central government initiative might require a gender balance, or the selectors might be more aware of women who stand out from the crowd of men.

Being noticed

One of the positive aspects of being a woman headteacher is being 'noticed' – their rarity value might open up unexpected opportunities:

> I do tend to be invited to working groups as the 'woman'.

> Because we are in a minority, I feel officers in the county make a conscious effort to involve us in county initiatives.

> It opens opportunities for my own development because there are so few female headteachers. Achievements are more readily noticed/recognised by colleagues within education for the same reason.

Again, the advantage lies in the women being perceived as different by gatekeepers who may be predominantly male. However, favouring women as rarities is unlikely to increase the numbers of women in headship or other positions of power. The rarity value factor might discourage some women headteachers from welcoming the entry of more women into senior positions. The 'queen bee' syndrome is recognised amongst women in power (Schmuck and Schubert, 1995, Blackmore,1999). Women who have made it may not wish to lose their special status and may resent others following them, 'pulling up the ladder behind them' (Wild, 1994).

A world where men hold most of the power and money can affect the women's behaviour. Some of the heads admitted to deliberately playing up their sexuality and attractiveness to further the school's interests.

Using 'feminine wiles'

A number of responses concerned the perception of the 'femaleness' of the headteachers in the eyes of males. Some of the women admitted that they knowingly turned on the charm and used feminine wiles to get their way.

> The Chief Education Officer is susceptible to feminine charm.

> With older men, I deliberately use appalling wiles.

> I'm a hypocrite! I use feminine tactics to get my own way – especially with the governors – as they are the ones who like a stereotypical image!

> (female heads)

The aim may be to obtain funds or goods for the school:

> Most people with available funds are men – I'm afraid I am occasionally guilty of what might be called feminine wheedling.

However, this playing on novelty value and charming susceptible men are countered by one highly positive outcome of the survey, the real freedom some headteachers experienced in operating as women.

Not constrained by male stereotype

Perceptions about their difference free the women from the normal stereotypes surrounding headteachers. They considered this freedom to be hugely advantageous. As one of them told me:

> Sometimes you can get away with things because you are a woman, because you are breaking new ground. ... I've worried about the amount of time I spend talking to staff but it is one of the best ways of moving things on and giving them confidence. Because there is no stereotype for women [heads] you can be more relaxed, it is not so stressful. (Coleman, 1996b, p.172)

This view was certainly shared by women heads in the survey:

> It is sometimes difficult for others to easily label you.

> Most male colleagues don't know how to deal with an Asian woman head-teacher.

Several mentioned that they felt being female allowed them to ask for help more easily, or that they were: 'less afraid of admitting ignorance or being tentative.' Several commented on how the change from a previous, traditional (male) head had been welcomed:

> Following an extremely autocratic male head, a complete change, with some sensitivity, was very helpful.

> My position as head followed a particularly macho (and disastrous) male head.

Freedom from the restricting aspects of the male head stereotype was welcomed:

> Not worrying about status/other people's image of me enables me to talk more directly with staff, and I hope makes me more approachable. I think this helps me to know what is really going on! It's an awful generalization, but I think women managers play fewer games. (female head, Coleman 1996b)

They reported having an easier relationship with other women (staff and mothers) and girls. This may be particularly advantageous with regard to the relationship with parents, since parental contact with school is generally through the mother.

Approachability

Although some men and indeed women resent being managed by women, as we have seen, there can be advantages for a woman in managing women staff, particularly in a girls' school:

> In dealing with girls only and a staff which is predominantly female, I have an understanding, that men could not have, of some issues. (female head)

Both parents and governors tend to regard a woman as more appropriate as head of a girls' school, but in any school, mothers of pupils and girl students may find a woman head more approachable:

> In dealing with parents. Generally, pupils are represented/accompanied by mothers/female guardians. They seem to find it easier to talk to another female. (female head)

The fact that some of the headteachers are mothers themselves and can understand the difficulties that parents and female staff may face is also seen as an advantage.

Empathy and emotion

Several of the heads referred to the particular skills of women in times of emotion, and their ability to empathize with others. This was mentioned in association with the trauma caused by the death of pupils or in cases of abuse or domestic violence. Again, they felt free of the 'male' stereotype of headship:

> It's easier to deal with emotions and to show feelings.

> Empathizing with distressed parents.

> I can touch children of either sex (a hug when upset) without people suggesting ulterior motives.

> (female heads)

Although she did not claim that only women are caring, one of the interviewed heads noted an additional freedom:

Men and women have the same qualities, but women are expected to be caring so they can be. Men can be just as caring. As a woman you can put your hand on someone's shoulder to reassure them, for a man that might be misinterpreted. (*ibid.*)

One of the most exciting outcomes of the survey was the recognition by some of the women that their existence both as insiders (the status of head) and as outsiders (women) gave them freedom to operate in ways that were not constrained by 'male' stereotypes of management and leadership.

Most of the men do not aspire to 'male' stereotypes. Both men and women see themselves as basically collaborative and people oriented. However, when it comes to examining why the women and men think they were successful in getting to headship, and by extension, how they think others can be successful, much more traditional thoughts dominate.

How can I make it to the top?

Although women may be able to relax and enjoy carrying out the role of headteacher in a way that is relatively free from some of the stereotypes surrounding headship, the route to headship is a different matter. There was no difference in the order and relatively little difference in the ratings that the men and women gave to a list of factors that they thought had contributed to their success.

Table 8.1: Reasons for success		
	all women %	**all men %**
Through hard work	84.9	81.1
Support from others	47.4	55.1
Knowing what you wanted	37.7	34.5
Academic ability	21.9	30.8

The vast majority of women and men thought that they earned their success through hard work. This meant signing up for a life style that involved long hours, after-school meetings and putting work before personal life much of the time. The interviewed heads bore this out describing sacrifices they had had to make to attain headship and, once there, to function successfully as a head. Such a life style does tend to demand the support of others to make up the shortfall of time to attend to personal matters. Men are more likely to see the support of others as important to their success. However, the remarks this question provoked showed that the men and the women were thinking about different forms of support. The men generally referred to their wife and family. Remember that they were much more likely to have partners that took major responsibility for home and family. The younger men in particular rate support from others highly and this group was the least likely to take on responsibilities in the home (see Chapter Five). However, the women saw support in terms of professional support and encouragement. It is the older women with children who rate support from others more highly than any of the other groups of women. As virtually all the children of these women are adult or near adult, and these women also tended to be responsible for domestic tasks, they are seldom talking about domestic support. The women spoke about career support and mentioned specific people who had supported them:

> Support of three excellent headteachers – all male – and most importantly my husband. (female head)

In *Dancing on the Ceiling*, Valerie Hall (1996) stresses the great importance of the support of both colleagues and husbands to the six headteachers that she observed and interviewed.

'Knowing what you wanted' was often rated as important by the women under 50 and all the women with children and far less so by other women and all the men. After all, choosing to be a headteacher and a mother does imply some planning and real determination. Men are generally more likely than women to mention their academic abilities as contributing to their career success, matched by only one group of women – the headteachers of girls' schools. This fits with the tradition of academic rigour and achievement in girls' schools.

Women heads for girls' schools
It was noted by men that women were more likely to be appointed heads of girls' schools, and some of the women respondents specified that a woman was preferred for the job:

Governors wished to have a female head as it is a school for girls.

A woman might be considered particularly suitable in other schools too:

> Being a 'good woman' can be advantage. I think my school was looking for a woman.

Heads of girls' schools rated 'Knowing what you wanted' least of any group. Career progression may be a little less hazardous in girls' schools. These schools are more likely actively to seek women heads than co-ed and boys' schools, and 15 per cent of the heads of girls' schools attributed their success to being a woman, whereas only eight per cent of the women from co-ed schools thought so.

The factor rated highest by all is 'hard work'. The determinants of success favoured by the headteachers of both sexes are those of the traditional male values associated with career progress. As well as rating the factors that they were given, nearly half the respondents gave additional reasons for their success. Are any of these to do with gender?

Being in the right place
A large number of the respondents, particularly the men, put their success down not to their own abilities but to 'being in the right place at the right time', or to 'circumstances' or simply 'luck':

> Right person in right place at right time plus natural abilities plus commitment to personal development. (male head)

However, the 'being in the right place at the right time' had a good deal to do with the ability to move, and this was greater for the male heads:

> Luck, prepared to move around, prepared to go into difficult schools. (male head)

The effect on wife and family and the difficulties of moving were mentioned by several:

> Demonstrated at each stage of my career that I could go further, made sacrifices (joint with family) to go where jobs were. (male head)

The women who mentioned luck as a factor in their success did not mean this in terms of the seizing of opportunities like the men did. Seizing opportunities in such a way often involved disruption to the family, something which women were less likely to do.

Self-confidence and personal qualities

One of the issues considered detrimental to women's success is their lack of self-confidence (see Chapter Two). Certainly, men were more than twice as likely as women to claim that it was their personal quality or qualities that led to their success, qualities that were often unconventional. One man said that he was 'not the usual type of candidate', another said he had 'nous', another claimed 'the ability to bullshit-quickly!' and another 'the ability to articulate my views in interview'. Yet another asserted that:

> I think quickly and clearly (most of the time!) and can usually handle six balls in the air. (male head)

The women who described personal qualities were less flamboyant, and typically identified traits that were much more mainstream and recognisable as appropriate for job descriptions or references:

> ...because I am competitive and have a certain kind of confidence.
>
> ...being clear, honest, making demands, – high expectations.
>
> Good organisation, being articulate and assertive, zest, sense of humour.
>
> (female heads)

However, the qualities most mentioned by both women and men related to the communication and 'people' skills, valued in the most popular style of management:

> ...the ability to understand, relate to, win trust of, inspire and manipulate colleagues. (female head)
>
> ...ability to build positive and trusting relationships with a wide range of people. (male head)
>
> People do not feel threatened by me. They see me as approachable. (male head)

Despite the popularity of 'feminine' management qualities, it was significant that some of the women linked their success to an ability to operate like a man as defined in the male stereotype of leadership.

Women conforming to male stereotypes

Tougher management skills were mentioned specifically by the women, which connects with the group of women who identified their management as autocratic/directive. This also supports the idea that some women feel they have to manage and lead in a stereotypically male way in order to succeed. One woman explained her success as engendered:

> ...by exhibiting qualities sometimes deemed to be 'masculine' – I am analytical, thorough, outspoken and sometimes seen as frightening by men. [My] hard definite views on what I wanted also helped. (female head)

Women gave the importance of determination a higher rating and this can be linked with the strong belief of many women that they 'need to prove their worth' and that women have to be 'twice as good as a man'. Several of the women commented on this:

> I have wanted to show that women can do well.

> I was often the only woman on the shortlist and being 'different' may have helped.

Even somewhat cynically:

> They needed a woman head – tokenism. I have a very forceful personality – a good male substitute maybe.

Having vision (Beare *et al* 1993) is most closely linked with leadership and the importance of this was stressed equally by both sexes.

Vision and values

All the headteachers were clear about the values they held. The following illustrate how they linked their values with their success:

> Being very clear about my own education values – eventually I found others who shared the same values. (male head)

> Having a strong sense of direction that communicates itself to others. (female head)

> I'm an enthusiast and it shows on interview. I believe passionately in the value of young people. (female head)

In some cases, the specific values were those of the Christian religion:

> My Christian faith bought me into education, to realise a vision for the young. As a head I can drive that forward more carefully. (female head)

> Having a clear vision of the purpose of Roman Catholic education. (male head)

While one of the men specifically mentioned a political ideology:

A desire to help establish an equitable society – something of a political ideology, attending a secondary modern school was/is a factor!

What are the factors that helped them make it?

The women and men headteachers in the survey were not very different in their rating of the factors that made them successful.

> The traditional routes to success identified with a typically male career pattern dominate, particularly the importance of hard work. However, there are some indications of differences. For women: the importance of support in the career and of determination and, in some cases, working in girls' schools. For men: the support of wife and family and the ability to take advantage of opportunities when they arise.

In addition, some of the women have, consciously or unconsciously, adopted typically masculine ways of operating in the school. When asked whether being a woman was an advantage for a headteacher, one woman answered that there was not and that...

If there was, I would not use it. Rational management is my tool.

Conclusion

The impact of gender on being a manager is much more likely to be perceived by women than men. Most of the women could relate their experience as headteacher to their gender and sexuality. Only a few of the men conceptualised their experience in the same way; the majority did not relate their work to their gender. Evetts (1994) comments on the way gender impinges on male and female heads' experiences:

For this woman head, gender was intrusive and prominent in her experience of headship. (p.92)

This is contrasted with the experience of men, for whom:

...their gender is positively associated with increased managerial responsibility and authority in their schools. (p.93)

Although awareness of gender is generally linked with inequity and seen as problematic for women, many of the women in the survey saw gender advantages in their role as headteacher. The female headteachers reported on benefits derived from their 'different' status, particularly the fact that they did not present an aggressive and challenging pose to angry males and therefore could disarm them. More importantly, they reported on the freedom that not complying with the male stereotype of leadership gave them, something that has also been noted in qualitative research with small numbers of female headteachers. Hall (1996) comments on the relative freedom from stereotypes that some women may experience, particularly when their father has been influential and supportive. They 'may be exposed to a more diverse set of role options than men, as a result of the different conceptualization of men and women's roles in society' (Hall, 1996, p.317). Possibly as a result of this, the female headteachers in the survey had been able to:

> ...develop an appreciation of their own feminine strengths and abilities that does not depend on male approval. None of the heads, either as child or adult, felt the need to be more like a boy or man in order to progress or win approval. (*ibid*. p.318)

Grogan (1996), reporting in the USA on 27 female aspirants to the superintendency, refers to their self-assessment of why they are good at their jobs. The responses fell into three categories: people skills, reflective approaches to management and 'the offer of alternative perspectives to problem solving and decision making' (p.138). She sums up her qualitative research with these women thus:

> It is clear in the narrative that women who have been constituted by the discourses of partnering and mothering in particular bring many of their relational strengths into their administrative practices. The data simply suggest that many of the women in this study would approach leadership from perspectives that have been influenced by experience different from those many men administrators have. (*ibid*. p.139)

Nevertheless, the headteachers in the survey were operating within a set of expectations where hard work was the most important determinant of success. The amount of hard work required causes some women to choose not to have children, and presumably deters others from applying for headship. The same pressures are overtly recognised by some of the men who refer to the 'price that has been paid' by them, and by their families.

Learning points for aspiring women:

- Despite the difficulties in getting there, being a woman headteacher has its advantages

- Women headteachers experience freedom to act outside the 'male' stereotypes of leadership

- Women have an advantage when dealing with aggressive males – confrontation is reduced

- While women are in the minority they benefit from 'getting noticed'

- Hard work is still seen as the key to success

- Career support and determination are also crucial

- Girls' schools prefer women heads.

Learning points for headteachers:

- Enjoy your relative freedom of action

- Use your status to encourage other women, even if it means your novelty value is decreased

- Offer career support to other women.

9

Do headteachers promote the career development of women?

The book started with a number of questions. Most were relevant to the women who might become heads in the future, while others related to the headteachers and other senior managers who are in post today. The learning points at the end of the chapters include points for both aspiring women and those headteachers currently in post. This chapter focuses on current headteachers and how they encourage the careers of teachers, particularly the women. The questions first identified in the introduction (p.viii) that relate to this chapter are:

- What career support and advice are we offering?
- Do we provide career mentoring?
- Are we offering appropriate role models?
- How do we view maternity leave?
- Are we family friendly?
- Are we aware of sexist behaviour?
- Are we feminists?

How do headteachers encourage the careers of teachers and especially women?

The headteachers of secondary schools in England and Wales in my survey are all in positions of power and are able to introduce and possibly institutionalise their personal vision in the school. They present themselves as caring individuals, in the way they perceive themselves as leaders and managers. However, few of them indicate any ways in which they might specifically support women staff, particularly those with young families.

The headteachers encouraged their staff to aim for promotion and career development solely through the normal channels of professional development, predominantly attendance at courses and receiving mentoring, although the provision of role models was commented on by a good many heads, both women and men. One to one activities like appraisal or special interviews with the headteacher or other member of the senior management team were also mentioned. A remarkable number of the heads, particularly the women, made a point of conducting one to one interviews with all their staff to discuss their needs and progress:

> ...very important to find time to have one to one conversations about individual strengths and needs.

> I interview all staff, teaching and support staff for 45 minutes each, in every spring term.

> (female headteachers)

Staff were also encouraged through whole-school programmes of staff development, through Investors in People and by offering specific opportunities, for instance to manage a short term project or take on additional responsibility. There were also suggestions about observation, shadowing, role rotation and peer review and a few heads provided practical means of encouragement such as practice interviews. One woman headteacher saw maternity leave as a development opportunity in a largely female school even though cover might be difficult, allowing for 'taking on 'acting' responsibilities during frequent maternity absences'.

Special encouragement for women?

Against this background of general encouragement and the professional development of all teachers, the heads were asked whether they did anything special to encourage the careers of women teachers. About two thirds (slightly more men than women) indicated that they did not treat women differently from men. They all, especially the women, seem anxious to be fair: 'equality of opportunity is the norm in this school!' (female headteacher); 'Why should there be a difference?' (male headteacher); 'There are only good teachers. All staff are treated as individuals and needs are met irrespective of gender.' (male headteacher)

Blackmore (1999) found that:

> Many women principals' primary criterion of judgement was that of fairness. In seeking to be transparently fair, they were constrained by the fear of being seen to favour women, and thus replicate the patriarchal school leadership in schools of old times. (p.190)

Some of the heads of girls' schools remarked that they did not treat the women differently because their staff was almost entirely female! However, the lack of distinction between the ways in which women and men encourage the career progress of female teachers is the general rule, except for a few men showing a rather 'patriarchal' and uninformed attitude:

> I confess, I had not considered this as a gender issue except in respect of roles for senior women.

> ...with the exception of those who I judge could make SMT level, there I give special attention.

> SMT targets individuals and encourages ambition.

> (male headteachers)

When all the comments are taken into account, about 40 per cent of the women and about 35 per cent of the men appear to take some action to ensure that women receive some form of career development that is tailored to their gender-specific needs. This could take the form of mentoring or encouragement of a particular kind, possibly one to one interviews:

> Women are encouraged more than men.

> The same as others but more, as confidence is often ridiculously low.

> (male headteachers)

Providing role models

When the headteacher is a woman, she often acknowledges her own importance as a role model and some also referred to the doubts and lack of confidence evidenced by their women staff:

> Personal conversation. I always encouraged competent women, from being an NQT onwards, making sure they see themselves as possible runners, and boosting their confidence.

> Individual discussion, also with male staff, but I find many women, although very good, do not have confidence to put themselves forward for promotion.
>
> (female headteachers)

The question of the role model was highly rated by all. They saw providing appropriate role models as a means of avoiding stereotyping. One woman head, for example, said she ensures that she has 'a high percentage of female role models, – SMT, heads of science and maths etc'. A number of the men spoke about ensuring that there were plenty of good female role models for their women staff:

> They have role models on the staff at all levels (except head and I can't do much about that!)

Although men may act as role models for women, there is evidence in management that female role models encourage the development of female managers:

> Numerous studies have shown that female role models in higher managerial positions act as important influences in terms of career aspirations for other women. (Davidson and Cooper, 1992, p.87)

Davidson and Cooper note that female role models can change the attitudes of both women and men, acting positively on males who, without the evidence, tend to doubt the ability of women to do well in a senior position. The importance of providing a role model for black women arises, as Elaine Foster relates:

> Many black colleagues contact me to ask for advice on their futures. As a black woman, I became tired of people implying that black people could not become heads. Being a role model in areas like Handsworth is also very important. (Hustler, et al 1995, p.39)

Women headteachers in the survey saw encouraging women through being a role model as important, particularly in the context of their domestic role:

> I talk to them about the issues, making it clear I have children etc. – i.e. trying to be a role model.

Such headteachers, having achieved a position of power, recognise the importance of acting as role models in their own right. The heads in Hall's (1996) study could be...

Prototypes of success in the current educational climate. As such, they emerge as and are expected to be role models for other women aspiring to leadership in schools and potentially for other men. (p.196)

However, these heads were setting high standards – and this caused some negative reactions, when they were seen as 'working excessively hard and setting personal standards that were sometimes hard for others to reach' (ibid. p.124). The example they set was almost too good: 'The almost superhuman qualities that the heads were often described as possessing and to which they aspired could potentially have been demotivating for others' (ibid. p.127). These heads were not able to draw any lessons from role models on how they might successfully combine work and family.

The heads I interviewed were also very conscious of the long hours they worked and could see no other way of carrying out the job.

Women only courses

About 20 per cent of the heads (a few more women than men) encouraged their female teachers to attend women only courses. Such courses included: women in management, assertiveness training, women's groups and women's conferences and local training courses. Several of the male headteachers mentioned the SHA course for female deputy heads.

The importance of formal and informal support for women by other women is indicated by researchers in the USA (Schmuck, 1995, Gupton and Appelt Slick, 1996). There, women's networks may be particularly identifiable in respect of the establishment of advocacy groups. In Australia, research indicates the importance of women's groups (Blackmore, 1994) and likewise networking and support is also recognised in the UK (Perry, 1993, Peace, 1994, Hustler, 1995). However, not all women feel the need for the support of other women. The subjects of Hall's (1996) study clearly felt that the support of colleagues and family was sufficient. The female headteachers in the survey rarely mention women's groups although those that are mentioned – such as the group of female secondary heads in North Yorkshire, Supporting Women in Secondary Schools (SWISS) – are much appreciated.

Handling maternity leave and returners

Issues such as the handling of maternity leave were considered and more radical help suggested, such as job sharing.

> Being flexible about moves between part-time and full-time. Job shares (though not yet at present school). (female headteacher)

> Finding opportunities for responsibility in a variety of ways – particularly important for returners. Enhancing the role of positive women in whole-school issues. (female headteacher)

> Providing equal opportunities and flexible/creative career break support. (male headteacher)

> Enabling part-time staff to hold full responsibility allowance posts and receive the full pay. (male headteacher)

There was one example of unofficial positive discrimination by a male head:

> We try not to draw any distinction. The strategies which we use at interview tend to mean that females are promoted in preference to males.

Whilst there is a commitment to staff development as a whole, it would appear that a substantial minority of the headteachers are aware of a need to foster the career progress of women separately. However, only a few have moved beyond courses and mentoring to actively encourage female staff in more radical and practical ways, such as job sharing and flexible work practices which might make return from maternity leave and combining work with looking after young children more feasible.

Certain women headteachers might have made a commitment to development of their women teachers in light of their own feminist ideas. But there is no evidence from the survey that the women head-teachers perceived society from a feminist perspective.

Headteachers and feminism

Blackmore (1999, p.57) comments on the mistaken 'conflation' of female leadership and feminism, and there is little evidence in the UK of any headteachers openly espousing feminism. There is a general un-labelled commitment to equality of opportunity and the recognition by some of the need for additional support and encouragement for women. In contrast, Blackmore (1999) reports on Australian women principals admitting to being feminist and Gatenby and Humphries (1999) and Strachan (1998) note women feminist leaders in New Zealand.

Grace (1995) researched headteachers in the North-east of England, and reports on the 'relative silence of these women headteachers on the gender relations of educational leadership and management' (p.188). He concludes that their 'silence' and unwillingness to espouse an openly feminist agenda in a region where men are exceptionally dominant means that:

> Patriarchal domination of school leadership positions had not been seriously threatened by the promotion of these women headteachers. They had been accommodated in what remained a largely enduring culture of male leadership. (p.190)

The unwillingness to openly espouse feminist values is found among many successful female educational managers. Matthews (1995) differentiates between the women leaders who fully support other women and those who deny that gender creates any difficulties in leadership. Research by Matthews (1995) identifies four types of women managers: 'activists' who seek to promote women within education; 'advocates' who support other women; 'isolates' who deny that discrimination exists and 'individualists' who take the view that it is the individual that matters, not their gender – these women tend to model themselves on male colleagues and to be rather judgmental about other women in senior management. The 'isolates' may acknowledge that some women experience discrimination but deny any personal knowledge of it. They are:

> Detached from issues of equity in administration. They have a certain naiveté about the problems of sex discrimination in educational administration. (Matthews, 1995, p.256)

It seems likely that most of the women in the survey who claimed to have had no experience of sexism could be categorised as 'individualists' or 'isolates'.

Matthews' 'activists' had typically been influenced by the women's movement, and considered supporting women colleagues as important. They questioned the *status quo* and were capable of being critically aware of the system and the place of women in it. There was little evidence of any 'activists' among the women headteachers surveyed. I did not specifically ask whether they would describe themselves as feminist, but nobody made overt statements about feminism. Indications of the difficulties women suspected of being feminist might face were revealed by two comments on the selection process:

> The Governors were apprehensive of appointing 'an assertive women' – a report back by an advisor!

> I was asked at interview for headship: 'as one of your references refers to you as Ms. Does this mean that you are aggressive?'

Most of the women and many of the men in the survey come closest in attitude to the 'advocates' category. In Matthews' terms they supported the idea of other women in school administration but aimed for a balance of men and women in senior positions. They valued relationships with both men and women and did not envisage a transformation of society.

Awareness of discrimination

Although the headteachers in the survey do not consciously view the world through a feminist lens, most of the women and some men were aware of sexism and gave examples from their professional experience. As we have seen, about two thirds of the women described sexist attitudes in the course of their work. But a third had not perceived encountering sexism. So quite a number would consider that there is 'no problem' (Schmuck, 1995) or are not as sensitised to the cultural context as the majority. These are likely to be older women, single or married without children, or working in girls' schools. The younger women, those who are married, and/or have children and work in a mixed or male environment are more likely to recognise gender bias even if they do not overtly espouse feminism.

For the men, the proportions relating to the perception of sexism are reversed: 66.6 per cent do not perceive sexist attitudes. Although just over half stated that they felt they had to prove their worth, this was almost always in relation to proving worth as a manager, not as a male manager. The notion: 'think male think manager' makes having to prove your worth as a male manager irrelevant.

The impact of location

Cutting across the perceptions is the 'London effect'. Women heads in London are less likely to mention having sexist peers than their female colleagues elsewhere in the country, particularly women from the shire counties and Wales. The London women are also less likely to feel that they must prove their worth. However, the opposite is true for the men headteachers in London, who are presumably sensitised to sexist attitudes and aware of keen competition from the women. They are more likely than male heads elsewhere to identify sexism in peers, have doubts about achieving headship and feel that they have to prove their worth.

Conclusion

The headteachers reported a range of activities in their schools that would enhance the career development of both women and men teachers. The predominant view was that gender was irrelevant to career development and that it might be seen as unfair if it did feature. However, more than a third recognised a need to provide additional support for women, usually because they perceived them as being less confident. Those who did recognise the need for additional support for women were concerned that they and others in the school were providing appropriate role models of women that cut across stereotypes. There are still a number of male heads who appear to be totally oblivious to gender issues and reveal a somewhat patriarchal attitude when asked about special career development for women.

Provision for career development is made against a background where two thirds of the women and one third of the men recognise the existence of sexism and where none are overtly espousing a feminist point of view.

Learning points for aspiring women:

* Only a minority of schools will specifically be considering the career development of women

* Courses, mentoring and appraisal are the most popular means of developing the careers of teachers. Women only courses are supported in about one fifth of schools

- In only a small minority of schools are radical measures considered that will specifically help women e.g. job-sharing.

Learning point for headteachers:

- Reconsider your approach to career development of teachers, particularly women teachers

- Think about more radical measures that could help women returners

- Be aware that children have two parents and cultivate the idea that both women and men have family responsibilities.

- Re-assess the meaning of feminism and allow yourself to see the world through a feminist lens.

10

Conclusions:
women in headship –
striking a balance

This final chapter relates the learning points that have emerged throughout the book to the practical and theoretical issues that affect women and specifically women in education who might wish to progress to senior management.

The book has been written from the viewpoint of women, taking issues that relate to gender and considering them in light of the responses of women and also men headteachers to a survey exploring career progress and management style. I sincerely hope that the book will be read by men as well as women, since the lessons that can be drawn from the research also apply to them as teachers, aspiring and actual senior managers and as family members, particularly fathers and husbands/ partners. 'Striking a balance' is the subtitle of the book and balance in professional and domestic life is good for everyone, women, men and families. The book explores the achievement of a balance between your personal and your professional life and within each part. It has indicated the relevant wider issues of balance in society and the imbalance epitomised by the relatively small numbers of women in leadership positions and the difficulties they face because of their gender.

What can we learn from the experience of the headteachers (women and men)?

One of the most important questions for women is 'Will I be up against institutionalised views that make my career progress difficult?'

The existence of traditional, stereotyped views about women, men and management is confirmed by the majority of women and some men headteachers. The women reported examples of overt, direct and indirect discrimination and even sexual harassment. A few men also commented on potential discrimination against men who do not conform to the stereotypical 'male' norm of headship. The message here is that despite a gradual increase in the numbers of women headteachers, basic attitudes are slower to change. Overt discrimination is now illegal, and in terms of equal opportunities, much has been done to ensure that women are not impeded in the blatant ways they were before the 1975 Sex Discrimination Act. However, feminist analysis reveals that society is basically still patriarchal. When I first began researching women headteachers, I visited China and I was sent an account of what it is like to be a woman academic in China. This brief extract sums up the difficulties faced by women in a society where men always have the advantage:

> Women and men are like two athletes running on the same track. But the men run free while the women balance children in one hand and kitchenware in the other. And even if the encumbered women run as fast as the men, people then criticise them for not running gracefully. (Fu Jun, 1995)

As this book ends I have to conclude that society here, as in China, is structured to favour men. However, the views of the British women headteachers were that it was best simply to ignore prejudice and discrimination when they encountered it and find a strategy for avoiding its impact. It is possible to disentangle some pragmatic advice from the experience of the women and men headteachers which may be relevant to those who work within the existing parameters even though it may not help to change society. In other words, while concluding that we live in a basically patriarchal society where change is slow, I suggest ways of operating within this context that can help the individual and also help to hasten change.

How can I make it to the top?

The career pattern the headteachers have followed is analogous to the race described so vividly by Fu Jun. Evans (1995) points out that this race may not include everybody, and its very existence is open to question:

> The race, that is, must indeed be to the swift, the battle to the strong. One sceptical feminist question, however, has been, how do we know who is the most swift, if some are excluded from the race? And an even more

sceptical one, not on the whole put forward by liberal feminists: why do we value so strongly, speed and strength? Indeed, why should we want a race? (p.31)

If we accept that we are in the race whether we want it or not, there is value in looking at what the headteachers did to win. And it is possible that those who participate in the race could subtly change the way it is run, or change how the winners behave. We have already seen that women headteachers feel freed of the male stereotype of leadership. Perhaps they can use some of that freedom in constructive ways for themselves, their schools and other aspiring heads.

One of the key elements that emerges from the experience of the head-teachers is that there are things that an individual can do which will help them in the race. Planning and being positive about a career; avoiding being pigeon-holed into a pastoral role and ensuring that you have a mentor are some strategies to bear in mind. However, without planning their career, many of the headteachers have 'drifted' into their roles, often seeming unaware of their own abilities. Certain people appear to have qualities that are recognised by others and which can lead to their being chosen for leadership positions. Even some of the women and men who have achieved headship seem to lack confidence.

However, determination and confidence are characteristic of many of the headteachers, and men in particular often have the confidence to apply for a job even if they do not have all the stated qualifications – something women might learn to emulate. And it is worth noting that more women than men have been appointed from the younger age group in recent years, so even if you think you may be too young, or in-sufficiently qualified for headship, the selection panel may think other-wise.

Women could think about the odds of being appointed head of a girls' school, which are far better than those for co-educational schools, al-though being head of a girls' school may carry less cachet than being head of a mixed school. Similarly, they could think about geography. Women are at least as likely as men to obtain headships in London, the nearer they are to the capital the greater are their chance of becoming a head. Trying to become a head in Scotland, Wales, the North East, South West or East Anglia, particularly in rural areas, increases the odds against women.

These are issues for women to consider when making their career plans, despite the institutionalised views about women in management and leadership positions. Barriers still exist, even though they are slowly being worn down.

Balancing work and family

Although an individual woman might be determined enough to go after headship and ignore assumptions about gender on the way, the reconciling of work and family is another matter. Here the experience of the headteachers is somewhat depressing. Faced with the difficulties, it seems that increasing proportions of the younger women headteachers are choosing not to have children. Following their example would probably mean opting to be childless. Although this choice is open to anyone, it is unlikely that more than 50 per cent of the age group would have made this choice unless circumstances impelled them. It appears that for women, combining children and headship is very difficult so many choose to have a career and not children. The introduction of maternity leave may in some ways have made things worse for women. This may seem illogical, but in reality allowing women a number of weeks off for childbirth does not solve the childcare problems. The fact that the older women headteachers had had more children than their younger counterparts seems to bear this out. They tended to have taken more time off but the younger women no longer regard this as an option, possibly because the existence of maternity leave has changed the general expectation of how women wanting a career will plan their lives. Comparing the experience of the older and younger women headteachers, it is clear that there has been a change. More of the younger women are opting for a 'male' pattern of career where children figure much less; they either have one child or none, or less frequently two, taking only minimal maternity leave.

There is also some evidence of change in career models and life style amongst the younger women headteachers and their husband/partners, based on equal regard for the work of each partner. They may, for example, take it in turns to be promoted. These couples are more likely to share domestic responsibility. However, this change does not represent a fresh view of gender status and equality amongst a younger age group since the experience of the young male headteachers is rather different. The younger men are more likely than their older peers to take very little responsibility in their household. For the most part, their wives are taking the traditional role and offering support to their husbands, potentially at the expense of their own careers. In Chapter Five I identified three patterns:

- 'Traditional or subjective', the pattern that many of the wives of the men headteachers seem to have adopted

- The 'mixed mode' which is more common among the older women headteachers, where essentially they do everything, have a career and carry most of the domestic responsibility

- 'Changing' to describe the dual career and dual domestic responsibility that is becoming more common amongst the younger women headteachers.

The changes relate to the ways that the younger women and their partners jointly plan their careers, not to the pattern of their working life. There is no evidence by either men or women of any deviation from the traditional male pattern of long working hours. Whilst this continues to be the case, women and men managers will have difficulty playing a full part in family life. The working hours adopted by successful managers puts enormous strain on the balance of work and family. The surveys reported in the book were of women and men headteachers only and while the perceptions of the men about their wives are to some extent revealed, what is missing are the views of all the women who have made decisions not to pursue headship. Although the book is about becoming a headteacher, and the particular difficulties that aspiring women may face, not every woman – or man – will consider becoming a headteacher to be the pinnacle of a career in education.

The balance between work and family is particularly delicate for women, who will usually take the major responsibility for childcare. There are indications of a different and more equal style of partnership amongst the younger female headteachers and their partners but the traditional division of roles is still the norm for the men. Moreover, 'greedy' jobs like being a headteacher are difficult for anyone to reconcile with a full family life. Although people may desire a better balance, it will need a sea change in thinking for it to be achieved.

A balance in work

The stereotype of the headteacher appears to be not only male but also the traditional disciplinarian, yet most of the headteachers see themselves as collaborative and people oriented. There is little difference between the genders about this, although there are actually slightly more women than men who identify themselves as operating in a stereotypically 'male' fashion and this is more common in the older women. Women and men headteachers generally perceive themselves to be operating in a way that eliminates the old gender stereotypes. There is little evidence to endorse the feminine and masculine paradigms and much to indicate that the old male model of management is largely irrelevant. There is also an implication that essentialist feminism, which would identify women as being nurturing and caring in a way that men are not, and therefore as superior, should be questioned. The headteachers themselves perceive stereotypical attitudes amongst members of their role set who seemed to anticipate a more authoritarian and traditional way of operating. This is understood by the heads to operate against women and against the non-traditional males.

The notion that the majority of the headteachers are now operating in a collaborative and people oriented style is based on self perception. A great deal of recent literature informing leadership stresses a transformational and empowering style of leadership, for example, Gronn, 1999, Day *et al*, 2000, Law and Glover, 2000. There is also a general perception that collegiality is the preferred management style (Bush, 1995, Wallace, 1989) to which headteachers should aspire. Headteachers may be affected by these current ideas in the *zeitgeist*. However, there is quite likely to be a gap between the headteachers' perceptions of what they are doing and what they are actually doing. For example, Kingman (1996) in her study of Hong Kong principals, found discrepancies between the principals' self-perception and how the principal was perceived by the teachers in the school, although the gap tended to be bigger for the men. The gap between what a principal claims and what they do may be seen in the extent to which they actually embed their principles and vision into the culture of the school. For example, Schein, (1997, p.231) differentiates between the 'formal statements of organizational philosophy, values and creed' and how these are put into practice in the management of people. Similarly, 'How leaders react to critical incidents and organizational crises' is likely to be a better indicator of their leadership style than the management systems they put into place.

My research is limited to the views of the headteachers themselves, but their reports on how they operate in a practical way (availability to staff, spending time out of their office) seems to show that they are working in an open way that would be likely to support a collaborative and people centred approach. Hall's (1996) study of six female heads looked at what the heads themselves had to say about their work and also observed them in action and took account of the views of those they worked with. She found the gap between what they said and what they did to be small:

> The testimony of those interviewed during the research mainly supported the heads' claims ... In each case, one or two examples were identified where the heads were perceived to have contravened their usual patterns of behaviour, but they were seen as exceptions rather than the rule. (p.146)

What is it like being a woman headteacher?

Most of what is written about being a headteacher or a senior manager in schools takes no account of the gender of the individuals concerned. All leadership theory was originally written as if there were 'no difference' and most of the empirical work in the UK on headteachers, with a few notable exceptions (Evetts, 1990, 1994; Ouston, 1993; Ozga, 1993; Hall, 1996) has also been written in this way. Where gender has been addressed there has sometimes been an underlying assumption that women operated entirely differently from men, adopting a more 'feminine' management style (Gray, 1993). Although the men and women headteachers surveyed see themselves as operating almost entirely similar management styles, there is no doubt from the evidence of the surveys that being a woman and a headteacher is a very different experience from being a man and a headteacher. Generally, men have no cause to question their status, and are accepted in it, whereas the women often have to explain that 'yes I am the headteacher' when asked by visitors who expect to see a besuited man. This trivial example of difference carries through into the ways that the women think, with most feeling that, as women, they have to justify themselves as managers. The dominant image of the leader and manager is of a male. Therefore women who take on the role of headteacher are constantly dealing with the inherent contradiction of being in a powerful position but at the same time not being what is expected. The evidence of sexist attitudes from colleagues and peers is strong, particularly the examples of male-dominated meetings of secondary heads. In addition, women heads may meet antipathy from male and female subordinates which may be directed at stereotypical presumptions about management style and leadership abilities.

One area in particular on which the women heads commented was their isolation as women in an environment where men remained the norm. In her study, Hall (1996) identifies the implicit contradiction that the heads needed to establish their formal authority while maintaining their 'acceptability' (p.188) as women. The marginality of women has long been recognised:

> When token women perform individual acts, these acts become loaded with extra symbolism because what individuals do is evaluated as a sign of how women perform. Token women, then, face special pressures. They get attention because of their high visibility, their differences are exaggerated by those in the main-stream, and they are more easily stereotyped than people found in greater proportion. (Biklen, 1980, p.16)

The isolation of the women headteachers is linked to the expectation of the leader, i.e. the headteacher, being male. Consequently, the women headteachers may feel like outsiders despite the fact that they have been legitimated in their appointment. One way in which women may experience vulnerability is in the way that they are judged physically as well as in terms of how they carry out their job. Hall (1996, p.100) observes that female headteachers are judged as school leaders but seen also as: 'a woman on show.' Selectors and governors felt free to remark on the physical appearance of the female candidates for headship, as comments made by the women headteachers about their selection reveal. Blackmore (1994) also notes that appearance, particularly their stature, can create difficulty for females in management positions. Commenting on the appointment of a new vice principal she points out the automatic advantages the archetypal male presence brings to leadership:

> She was short and slight in build, and was seen to 'lack' the same presence of the previous Vice Principal who was strong, highly macho and a strict disciplinarian. He personified the traditional connections between

aggression, masculinity and good leadership (Blackmore 1993), and all staff in their interviews (over 35 interviews) mentioned the power of his presence in the school. (Blackmore 1994, p.13)

My survey established that women and men headteachers generally see themselves as having the same management style and values. However, observing their actions and particularly their speech might reveal differences related to their direct experiences of socialisation. There is clear research evidence to show that women use communication patterns that differ to those commonly found in men. For example women's conversation with other women tends to be supportive and responsive rather than engaging in the point by point debate more typical of male dialogue. Women's speech also tends to be more tentative (Shakeshaft, 1989, Schick-Case, 1994), leading male colleagues to judge them negatively. Whilst the survey does not lend itself to examination of spoken communication, some of the heads commented on the advantage of being a woman in dealing with girls, female staff and mothers. They are seen as being more approachable by other women, and the mother is the parent who tends to have dealings with the school. Similarly, the women headteachers felt freer to share emotion in unhappy circumstances and empathise with families where tragedies had occurred, in a way that men might find more difficult. This was true of the interviewed heads as well as those in the survey.

In some ways the most exciting finding of the survey is that women headteachers feel that they can conduct themselves in ways that are free of the expectations held of their male colleagues. Although the survey shows that men and women endorse the same management style, the cultural and social expectations surrounding the leadership of schools and other organisations continue to endorse the idea of the male as leader. Although male headteachers may see themselves as caring and tolerant, this is not the image of a headteacher stereotypically held by parents, students or governors. So it is the men who are in some ways trapped by a stereotype that places the majority of them in a straitjacket of expectations of male dominance, of which women headteachers are free.

So the answer to the question, 'What is it like to be a woman headteacher?' is at least partly that it is liberating for them both as women and in their professional role. They are freer than their male colleagues to explore the role and find their own ways of interpreting it.

What can existing headteachers learn about striking a balance?

Many of the learning points for headteachers listed at the end of each chapter refer to the ability of the headteacher to influence the culture of their school. The headteachers are urged to consider the staffroom culture and to be aware of the extent of hidden prejudices. The heads were very conscious of their importance as role models in the school and that messages they put across are likely to be clearly received. For example, it is important for the head to offer management opportunities to women as well as men, and to value pastoral experience (often identified with women) equally with a curriculum role (more often identified with men).

One way of having an impact on the wider culture is to ensure that certain instrumental procedures are in place, for example institutionalised mentoring and appraisal that considers career development, and that governors receive equal opportunities training.

In pursuit of balance in working and family life, headteachers should recognise that family ties for both women and men are to be respected and that responsibilities accrue to both parents. A more creative approach to maternity leave, returners and job sharing would be helpful to women when their children are very young. Similarly recognition of the skills and experience women accrue when looking after a family would help to set the balance straight. Drake and Owen (1998) quote an example from the diary of a woman principal in the USA:

> The sum of these life experiences causes me to reflect. I was the sole carer for my grandmother, my mother and my father. I shared responsibility for my mother-in-law and my father-in-law.... Were all these experiences, feelings and insights my true training for the principalship? Organising, managing and distributing time and resources were lessons learned. (p.136)

Valuing being a woman in a management role is a lesson that comes clearly from the research data. It would be a valuable experience for many of the heads of both sexes to stand back and make use of the experiences of women and re-interpret the world from their standpoint.

A better balance?

There is a slight increase in the number of women headteachers, but society seems reluctant to move towards equal numbers of women and men in management and leadership, notwithstanding the equal opportunities legislation of the 1970s. Blackmore (1999, pp.103-4) regards equal opportunities legislation as: 'a necessary but not sufficient condition for gender equity'. Commenting on the Australian experience, which has included affirmative action, she felt that the programme ensuring that women were preferred for appointment and that women with feminist beliefs were appointed to senior positions (the so called femocrats) failed to change the 'culturally embedded aspects of gender power relations'. It is unlikely that further legislation, government action and a simple increase in the number of women in senior positions will be enough to eliminate stereotypes or radically change the power structure of society.

Yet I have some sympathy with the equal opportunities approach, what Blackmore (1999, p.210) calls 'tactical' or 'sensible' feminism. The proportion of women in leadership is slowly growing. The recognition of the importance of role models and mentoring by both men and women is also a positive sign. The women headteachers in the survey had generally avoided being stereotyped in a pastoral role and a significant minority of the headteachers offered career development strategies of some kind for women teachers. Many of the male headteachers showed awareness of the difficulties faced by women, although a few felt that women were being favoured to the detriment of men. Affirmative action has never been UK policy but rights are slowly being instituted that allow for paternity leave. There is evidence of more young women taking on management roles and of firms valuing what they bring. Writing about work in general, and a management style appropriate to the present and future needs of business and industry, Handy (1994) speculates that:

> Organisations want quality people, well educated, well skilled and adaptable. They also want people who can juggle with several tasks and assignments at one time, who are more interested in making things happen than in what title or office they hold, more concerned with power and influence than status. They want people who value instinct and intuition as well as analysis and rationality, who can be tough but also tender, focused but friendly, people who can cope with these necessary

contradictions. They want, therefore, as many women as they can get. (p.179)

However, despite the expression of such eminently sensible views, a culture remains in which men are automatically seen as leaders and women are somehow judged as inferior and feel that they have to prove their worth.

What about the balance in our work and family lives? The experience of the women headteachers in the sample is testament to the difficulties of combining a management job with family life. The male headteachers, too, talk about the demands their job makes on their families. Anderson (1998) claims that in both public and private sectors, people are working the equivalent of a month a year more than they did 20 years ago. Such a work climate is not conducive to the demands of family life, particularly for women, on whom most of the demands, responsibilities and challenges still fall. The women headteachers under 50 are more likely to be married than their older colleagues, although still much less likely than the men to be married. There is evidence of them operating a balancing strategy, running dual career households, and being virtually equal to their husbands in terms of work life balance. However, the demands of job and family have meant that many more of them have chosen not to have children or to have only one.

A radical feminist approach would challenge the male structures of society and the current emphasis on the work ethic and somehow re-structure the ways men and women view the world. This would require the elimination of the binary view that places men on the rational positivist side of the public world and women on the emotional intuitive side of the domestic, and where the latter is considered innately inferior and women who cross the divide are subject to critical scrutiny.

There is no radical feminist consensus on how to move forward. Black-more (1999) stresses the continuing importance of the state in bringing about gender equity reform and advocates widening the debate to include all issues of inequality and justice. Individual commentators take particular stances. Kelly (2000, p.8) finds post-modernism 'in-adequate when it comes to changing the lives of half the world's population – namely women', and adopts instead a radical Marxist viewpoint. Davies (1998), having researched men and women in leadership in the developing world, considers that, although there is a dominant form of masculinity, both men and women are liberated by working within a democratic structure and schools that are based on democratic values:

> Gender interests are best served not by having more women 'at the top' but by having structures in place which promote equity and by having people of both sexes who believe in and abide by those structures. (Davies, 1998, p.24)

The survey findings show, perhaps unexpectedly, that there is something of a consensus among the headteachers on management style and that the favoured style is one that values people and collaborative approaches – and is the style that is labelled 'feminine'. This could be interpreted as a maintenance by men of the power structure, now they see that the values and styles identified as characteristic of women are simply ways of good management and have decided to take over the style now that it is popular.

However, the enthusiasm for collaborative management style signals a change in management and leadership values towards considering people's needs. Such a change may help to nurture a better gender balance in schools and in wider society. However, it is likely to be a some time before either the slow drip of change or a more radical reformulation of stereotypes and conceptualisations encompassing work, home and family means that a balance between women and men as leaders is truly achieved.

References

Acker, S. (1994) *Gendered Education*, Buckingham, Open University Press.

Acker, S. (1999) *The Realities Of Teachers' Work: never a dull moment*, London, Cassell.

Adler, N.J. (1994) 'Competitive frontiers: women managing across borders', *Journal of Management Development*, Vol. 13, No. 2., pp.24 – 41.

Adler, S., Laney, J. and Packer, M. (1993) *Managing Women: feminism and power in educational management*, Buckingham, Open University Press.

Al Khalifa, E. (1992) 'Management by halves: women teachers and school management', in Bennett, N., Crawford, M. and Riches, C. (eds.) *Managing Change in Education: individual and organizational perspectives*, London, Paul Chapman.

Alimo-Metcalfe, B. (1994a) 'Gender bias in the selection and assessment of women in management', in Davidson, M. and Burke, R. (eds.) *Women in Management: current research issues*, London, Paul Chapman.

Alimo-Metcalfe, B. (1994b) 'Waiting for fish to grow feet! Removing organizational barriers to women's entry into leadership positions, in Tanton, M. (ed.) *Women in Management*, London, Routledge.

American Association of School Administrators (1992) *Women and Minorities in School Administration: Facts and figures 1989-1990*.

Anderson, P. (1998) 'Choice: can we choose it?', in Radford, J. (ed.) *Gender and Choice in Education and Occupation*, London, Routledge.

Atkinson, P., Delamont, S. and Hammersley, M. (1993) 'Qualitative research traditions', in Hammersley, M. (ed.) *Educational Research: current issues*, London, Paul Chapman.

Bass, B.M. (1981) *Stogdill's Handbook of Leadership: a survey of theory and research*, Glencoe, Free Press.

Beare, H. Caldwell, B, and Millikan, R. (1993) 'Leadership', in Preedy, M. (ed.) *Managing the Effective School*, London, Paul Chapman.

Belbin, R.M. (1981) *Management Teams: why they succeed or fail*, Oxford, Heinemann Professional Publishing Ltd.

Bell, C. D. (1996) 'If I weren't involved with schools, I might be radical', in Dunlap, D. and Schmuck P.A. (eds.) *Women Leading in Education*, Albany, N.Y., State University of New York Press.

Bem, S.L. (1974) 'The measurement of psychological androgyny', *Journal of Consulting and Clinical Psychology*, 42 (2) pp 155-62.

Bem, S.L. (1977) 'On the utility of alternative procedures for assessing psychological androgyny', *Journal of Consulting and Clinical Psychology*, Vol. 45, No. 2, pp 196-205.

Bensimon, E. and Marshall, C. (1997) 'Policy analysis for post-secondary education: feminist and critical perspectives', in Marshall, C. (Ed.) *Feminist Critical Policy Analysis: a perspective from post-secondary education*, London, Falmer Press.

Biklen, S. K. and Brannigan, M. B. (1980) *Women and Educational Leadership*, Lexington, Lexington Books.

Blackmore, J. (1989) 'Educational leadership: a feminist critique and reconstruction', in Smyth, I. and John, W. (eds.) *Critical Perspectives on Educational Leadership*, Deakin Studies in Education Series 2, Lewes, Falmer Press.

Blackmore, J. (1994) 'Leadership in 'crisis': feminist insights into change in an era of educational restructuring', paper presented at the conference of the American Educational Research Association, New Orleans, April.

Blackmore, J. (1995) 'Breaking out from a masculinist politics of education', in Limerick, B. and Lingard, B. (eds) *Gender and Changing Educational Management*, Rydalmere, NSW, Hodder Education.

Blackmore, J. (1999) *Troubling Women: feminism, leadership and educational change,* Buckingham, Open University Press.

Bolam, R. *et al* (1993) *Effective Management in Schools: a report for the Department for Education via the School Management Task Force Professional Working Party*, London, HMSO.

Burke, R.J., and McKeen, C.A. (1994) 'Career development among managerial and professional women', in *Women in Management: current research issues*, London, Paul Chapman.

Burns, J.M. (1978) *Leadership*, New York, Harper and Row.

Bush, T., West-Burnham, J. and Glover, D. (1995) *Leadership and Strategic Management*, London, Pitman.

Bush, T. *et al* (1996) 'Mentoring and continuing professional development', in McIntyre, D. and Hagger J., (eds.) *Mentors in Schools: developing the profession of teaching*, London, David Fulton.

Cartwright, S. and Gale, A. (1995) 'Project management: different gender, different culture?', *Leadership and Organization Development Journal,* Vol. 16, no. 4, pp.12 – 16.

Charlesworth, K. (1997) *A Question of Balance? A survey of managers' changing professional and personal roles*, London, Institute of Management.

Coleman, M. (1994) 'Women in educational management', in Bush T. and West-Burnham J. (eds.) *The Principles of Educational Management*, Harlow, Longman.

Coleman, M. (1996a) 'Barriers to career progress for women in education: the perceptions of female headteachers', *Educational Research* Vol. 38 No 3, pp.317-332.

Coleman, M. (1996b) 'Management style of female headteachers', *Educational Management and Administration*, Vol. 24, No. 2, pp.163-74.

Coleman, M. (1997) 'Managing for Equal Opportunities: the gender issue', in Bush, T. and Middlewood, D. (eds.) *Managing People in Education*, London, Paul Chapman.

Coleman, M., Qiang, H. and Yanping, L. (1998) 'Women in educational management in China: experience in Shaanxi Province', *Compare*, Vol. 8, No. 2. pp.141-154.

Collinson, D. and Hearn, J. (1996) 'Breaking the silence: on men, masculinities and managements', in Collinson, D. and Hearn, J. (Eds.) *Managers as Men: Managers as Men*, London, Sage Publications.

Collinson, D. and Hearn, J. (2000) 'Critical studies on men, masculinities and managements' in Davidson, M. and Burke, R. (eds.) *Women in Management: current research issues volume II*, London, Sage Publications.

Cooper, C.L. and Lewis, S. (1995), 'Working together: men and women in organizations', *Leadership and Organization Development Journal,* Vol. 16, No. 5, pp.29-31.

Cooper, G. (1996) 'Corporate relocation policies', in Lewis, S. and Lewis, J. (eds.) *The Work-Family Challenge: rethinking employment,* London, Sage.

Coser, L. (1974) Greedy Institutions: patterns of undivided commitment, New York, The Free Press.

Cunnison, S. (1989) 'Gender joking', in Acker, S. (Ed.) *Teachers Gender and Careers,* Lewes, Falmer Press.

Darling, J. and Glendinning, A, (1996) *Gender Matters in Schools,* London, Cassell.

David, M.E. (1988) 'Prima Donna inter pares? women in academic management', in Acker, S. (ed.) *Teachers, Gender and Careers,* London, Falmer Press.

Davidson, M.J. and Cooper, C.L. (1992) *Shattering the Glass Ceiling: the woman manager,* London, Paul Chapman.

Davidson, M. (1997) *The Black and Ethnic Minority Manager: cracking the concrete ceiling,* London, Paul Chapman.

Davies, L (1990) *Equity and Efficiency? school management in an international context,* London, Falmer Press.

Davies. L. and Gunawardena, C. (1992) *Women and men in educational management: an international inquiry,* IIEP Research Report No. 95, Paris, International Institute for Educational Planning.

Davies, L. (1998) 'Democratic practice, gender and school management', in Drake, P. and Owen, P. (eds.) *Gender and Management Issues in Education: an international perspective,* Stoke on Trent, Trentham Books.

Day, C. *et al* (2000) *Leading Schools in Times of Change,* Buckingham, Open University Press.

Delamont, S. (1990) *Sex Roles and the School,* London, Routledge.

DfEE (2000a) *Statistics of Education Teachers in England and Wales,* London, Government Statistical Service.

DfEE (2000b) *Work Family Balance,* London, HMSO.

Dimmock, C. (2000) *Designing the Learning Centred School: a cross cultural perspective,* London, Falmer Press.

Drake, P. and Owen, P. (eds.) (1998) *Gender and Management Issues in Education: an international perspective,* Stoke on Trent, Trentham Books.

Education (1993) 'Women beware women on the way up', *Education,* 27 August.

Edwards, S. and Lyons, G. (1994) 'Female secondary headteachers – an endangered species?', *Management in Education,* Vol. 8, No. 2. pp.7 – 10.

Evans, J. (1995) *Feminist Theory Today: an introduction to second-wave feminism,* London, Sage.

Evetts, J. (1990) *Women in Primary Teaching: career contexts and strategies,* London, Unwin Hyman.

Evetts, J. (1991) 'The experience of secondary headship selection: continuity and change', *Educational Studies,* Vol. 17, No. 3, pp.285-94.

Evetts, J. (1994) *Becoming a Secondary Headteacher,* London, Cassell.

Faulstich-Wieland, H. (1997) 'The Federal Republic of Germany', in Wilson, M. (ed.) *Women in Educational Management: a European perspective,* London, Paul Chapman.

Fave-Bonnet, M. (1997) 'France', in Wilson, M. (ed.) *Women in Educational Management: a European perspective,* London, Paul Chapman.

Ferrario, M. (1994) 'Women as managerial leaders', in Davidson, M. J. and Burke, R. J. (eds.) *Women in Management: current research issues*, London, Paul Chapman.

Fu Jun, (1995) 'The problems Chinese professional women are faced with' in *Women's Studies*, Vol. 5, Ginling College, Beijing (in Chinese)

Gatenby, B. and Humphries, M. (1999) 'Exploring gender, management education and careers: speaking in the silences', *Gender and Education*, Vol. 11, No. 3, pp.281 – 294.

Gilligan, (1982) *In a Different Voice*, London, Harvard University Press.

Goffee, R. and Nicholson, N. (1994) 'Career development in male and female managers – convergence or collapse?' in Davidson, M. J. and Burke, R. J. (eds.) *Women in Management: current research issues*, London, Paul Chapman.

Gold, A. (1993) 'Women-friendly' management development programmes', in Ouston, J. (ed.) *Women in Education Management*, Harlow, Longman.

Gold, A. (1996) 'Women into educational management', *European Journal of Education*, Vol. 31, No. 4, pp.419 – 433.

Goldring, E. and Chen, M. (1994) 'The feminization of the principalship in Israel: the trade-off between political power and cooperative leadership', in Marshall, C. (ed.) *The New Politics of Race and Gender*, London, Falmer Press.

Gosetti, P.P. and Rusch, E. (1995) 'Re-examining educational leadership: challenging assumptions', in Dunlap, D. and Schmuck P.A. (eds.) *Women Leading in Education*, Albany, N.Y., State University of New York Press.

Grace, G. (1995) *School Leadership*, London, Falmer Press.

Grant, R. (1989) 'Women teachers' career pathways: towards an alternative model of 'career'', in Acker, S. (ed.) *Teachers, Gender and Careers*, London, Falmer Press.

Gray, H.L. (1993) 'Gender issues in management training', in Ozga, J. (ed.) *Women in Educational Management*, Buckingham, Open University Press.

Grogan, M. (1996) *Voices of Women Aspiring to the Superintendency*, Albany, N.Y., State University of New York Press.

Gronn, P. (1999) *The Making of Educational Leaders*, London, Cassell.

Gross, N. and Trask, A. (1976) *The Sex Factor and the Management of Schools*, New York, John Wiley and Sons.

Grundy, S. (1993) 'Educational leadership as emancipatory praxis', in Blackmore, J. and Kenway, J. (eds.) *Gender Matters in Education Administration and Policy: a feminist introduction*, London, Falmer Press.

Gupton, S. L. and Appelt Slick, G. (1996) *Highly Successful Women Administrators: the inside stories of how they got there*, Thousand Oaks, California, Corwin Press Inc.

Hall, T. (1976) *Careers in Organizations*, Santa Monica, CA., Goodyear.

Hall, V. (1993) 'Women in educational management: a review of research in Britain', in Ouston, J. (ed.) *Women in Education Management*, Harlow, Longman.

Hall, V. (1996) *Dancing on the Ceiling: a study of women managers in education*, London, Paul Chapman.

Hall, V. (1997) 'Dusting off the phoenix: gender and educational leadership revisited', *Educational Management and Administration*, Vol. 25, No. 3, pp.309 – 324.

Hall, V., Mackay, H. and Morgan, C. (1986) *Headteachers at Work*, Buckingham, Open University Press.

Handy, C. (1994) *The Empty Raincoat*, London, Hutchison.

Hellriegel, D., Slocum, J. W. and Woodman, R. W, (1992) *Organizational Behavior*, St. Paul, West Publishing Company.

HESA (Higher Education Statistics Agency) (2000) *Resources of Higher Education Institutions 1999/2000*, Cheltenham, HESA.

Hill, M. S. and Ragland, J.C. (1995) *Women as Educational Leaders: opening windows, pushing ceilings*, Thousand Oaks, California, Corwin Press, Inc.

Hurley, A.E. and Fagenson-Eland, E. (1996) 'Challenges in cross-gender mentoring relationships: psychological intimacy, myths, rumours, innuendoes and sexual harassment', *Leadership and Organization Development Journal*, Vol. 17, no 3, pp 42-9.

Hustler, D., Brighouse, T. and Ruddock J. (eds.) (1995) *Heeding Heads: secondary heads and educational commentators in dialogue*, London, David Fulton.

Jirasinghe, D. and Lyons, G. (1996) *The Competent Head: a job analysis of heads' tasks and personality factors,* London, Falmer Press.

Jones, A. (1987) *Leadership for Tomorrow's Schools*, Oxford, Blackwell.

Kelly, J. (2000) 'Gender and equality: one hand tied behind us', in Cole, M. (ed.) *Education, Equality and Human Rights*, London, Routledge/Falmer.

Kerfoot, and Knights (1995) 'The best is yet to come? Searching for embodiment in managerial work', in Collinson, D. and Hearn J. (eds.) *Masculinity and Management*, London, Sage.

Kingman, A. (1996) A Gender Study on Leadership: the female and male principals of Hong Kong secondary schools as perceived by teachers and the principals themselves, unpublished PhD thesis, University of Hong Kong.

Kotecha, P. (1994) 'The position of women teachers', *Agenda*, No. 21.

Kram, K. (1983) 'Phases of the mentor relationship', *Academy of Management Journal*, Vol. 26, No. 4, pp.608 – 25.

Kruger, M. L. (1996) 'Gender issues in school headship: quality versus power?', *European Journal of Education*, Vol. 31, No. 4, pp.447 – 461.

Law S. and Glover, D. (2000) *Educational Leadership and Learning: practice, policy and research,* Buckingham, Open University Press.

Lewis, S. (1994) 'Role tensions and the dual career couple', in Davidson, M. and Burke, R. (eds.) *Women in Management: current research issues*, London, Paul Chapman.

Lewis, S. (1996) 'Rethinking employment: an organizational culture change framework', in Lewis S. and Lewis, J. (eds.) *The Work-Family Challenge: rethinking employment*, London, Sage.

Lingard, B. and Douglas, P. (1999) *Men Engaging Feminisms: pro-feminism, backlashes and schooling,* Buckingham, Open University Press.

Litawski, R. (1992) The Role of the Female Deputy Head: an investigation into the role of the female deputy head in co-educational, maintained comprehensive schools, University of Loughborough, unpublished doctoral thesis.

Lumby, J. and Tomlinson, H. (2000) 'Principals speaking: managerialism and leadership in further education', *Research in Post-Compulsory Education*, Vol. 5, No. 2, pp.139-51.

Lynch, K. (1997) 'Ireland', in Wilson, M. (ed.) *Women in Educational Management: a European perspective*, London, Paul Chapman.

Mac an Ghaill, M., (1994) *The Making of Men: masculinities, sexualities and schooling*, Buckingham, Open University Press.

McBurney, E. G., and Hough, J. (1989) 'Role perceptions of female deputy heads', in *Educational Management and Administration*, Vol. 17, pp.115-18.

McMullan, H. (1993) 'Towards women-friendly schools', in Ouston, J. (ed.) *Women in Education Management*, Harlow, Longman.

Marshall, C. (1997) 'Dismantling and reconstructing policy analysis', in Marshall, C. Feminist *Critical Policy Analysis: a perspective from primary and secondary schooling*, London, Falmer Press.

Matthews, E.N. (1995) 'Women in educational administration: views of equity', in Dunlap, D. and Schmuck P.A. (eds.) *Women Leading in Education*, Albany, N.Y., State University of New York Press.

Middlewood, D. (1997) 'Managing recruitment and selection', in Bush, T. and Middlewood, D. (eds.) *Managing People in Education*, London, Paul Chapman.

Morgan, C., Hall, V. and Mackay, H. (1983) *The Selection Of Secondary School Headteachers*, Milton Keynes, Open University Press.

Morgan, V., Mason, C. and Scott, P. (1995) *Climbing the ladder: vertical segregation in nursing and teaching*, Equal Opportunities Commission for Northern Ireland.

Morris, S.B. Coleman, M. and Low, G.T. (1999) 'Leadership stereotypes and female Singaporean principals' *Compare*, Vol. 29, No. 2, pp.191-202.

Mortimore, P. and Mortimore, J. (1991) *The Secondary Head*, London, Paul Chapman.

Munro, P. (1998) *Subject to Fiction*, Buckingham, Open University Press.

Nelson-Jones (1986) *Human Relationship Skills*, London, Cassell.

Noddings, N. (1984) *Caring: a feminine approach to ethics and moral education*, Berkeley, University of California Press.

ONS (Office for National Statistics) *Social Trends 2001*, London, The Stationery Office.

Ouston, J. (ed.) (1993) *Women in Education Management*, Harlow, Longman.

Ozga, J. (ed.) (1993) *Women in Educational Management*, Buckingham, Open University Press,.

Peace, C. (1994) 'For those with a head for heights' in *Times Educational Supplement*, 1 September.

Perry, P. (1993) 'From HMI to polytechnic director' in Ozga, J. (Ed.) *Women in Educational Management*, Buckingham, Open University Press.

Pringle, J. and Timperley, H. (1995) 'Gender and educational management in New Zealand: cooption, subversion or withdrawal?', in Limerick, B. and Lingard, B. (eds.) *Gender and Changing Educational Management*, Rydalmere, NSW, Hodder Education.

Reay, D. and Ball, S. (2000) 'Essentials of female management', *Educational Management and Administration*, Vol. 28, No. 2, pp.145 – 160.

Restine, L. Nan, (1993) *Women in Administration: facilitators for change*, Newbury Park, California, Corwin Press Inc.

Ribbins, P. (ed.) (1997) *Leaders and Leadership in the School*, College and University, London, Cassell.

Riehl, C. and Lee, V.E., (1996) 'Gender, organizations, and leadership', in Leithwood, K., Chapman, J., Corson, D., Hallinger, P. and Hart, A. (eds.) *International Handbook of Educational Leadership and Administration*, Boston, Kluwer Academic.

Rowan, P. (1995) 'Gender issues and management styles', in Hustler, D., Brighouse, T. and Ruddock J. (eds.) (1995) *Heeding Heads: secondary heads and educational commentators in dialogue*, London, David Fulton.

Ruijs, A. (1993) *Women Managers In Education – A Worldwide Progress Report*, Bristol, the Staff College, Coombe Lodge Report.

Santos, M. (1997) 'Spain' in Wilson, M. (ed.) *Women in Educational Management: a European perspective*, London, Paul Chapman.

Schein, E.J. (1997) *Organisational Culture and Leadership*, 2nd Edition, San Francisco, Jossey-Bass.

Schein, V.E. (1994) 'Managerial sex typing: a persistent and pervasive barrier to women's opportunities', in Davidson, M. and Burke, R. (eds.) in *Women in Management: current research issues*, London, Paul Chapman.

Schick-Case, S. (1994), 'Gender differences in communication and behaviour in organizations', in Davidson, M. J. and Burke, R. J. (eds.) *Women in Management: current research issues*, London Paul Chapman.

Schmuck P.A. (1980) 'Changing women's representation in school management', in Biklen, S. K. and Brannigan, M. B. (1980) *Women and Educational Leadership*, Lexington, Lexington Books.

Schmuck, P.A. (1986) 'School management and administration: an analysis by gender', in Hoyle, E. and McMahon, A. (eds.) *The Management of Schools*, World Year-book of Education 1986, London, Kogan Page.

Schmuck, P.A. (1995) 'Advocacy organizations for women school administrators', in Dunlap, D. and Schmuck P.A. (eds.) *Women Leading in Education*, Albany, N.Y., State University of New York Press.

Schmuck, P.A. (1996) 'Women's place in educational administration: past, present, and future', in Leithwood, K., Chapman, J., Corson, D., Hallinger, P. and Hart, A. (eds.) *International Handbook of Educational Leadership and Administration*, Boston, Kluwer Academic.

Sedgewick, M. (1993) 'The secondary head', in Ozga, J. (ed.) *Women in Educational Management*, Buckingham, Open University Press.

Shakeshaft, C. (1989) *Women in Educational Administration*, Newbury Park, Sage.

Shakeshaft, C. (1993) 'Women in educational management in the United States', in Ouston, J. (ed.) *Women in Education Management*, Harlow, Longman.

Still, L. (1995) 'Women in management: glass ceilings or slippery poles?', in Limerick, B. and Lingard, B. (eds.) *Gender and Changing Educational Management*, Rydalmere, NSW, Hodder Education.

Stott, C. and Lawson, L. (1997) *Women at the Top in Further Education*, FEDA Report, London, FEDA.

Strachan, J. (1998) 'Feminist educational leadership in a New Zealand neo-liberal context', *Journal of Educational Administration*, Vol. 37, No. 2., pp.121 – 138.

Usher, P. (1996) 'Feminist approaches to research', in Scott, D. and Usher, R. (eds.) *Understanding Educational Research*, London, Routledge.

van Eck, E., Volman, M. and Vermeulen, A. (1996) 'The management route: analysing the representation of women in educational management', *European Journal of Education*, Vol. 31, No. 4, pp.403 – 417.

Vermeulen, A. and Ruijs, A. (1997) 'The Netherlands', in Wilson, M. (ed.) *Women in Educational Management: a European perspective*, London, Paul Chapman.

Vinkenburg, C., Jansen, P. and Koopman, P. (2000) 'Feminine leadership – a review of gender differences in managerial behaviour and effectiveness', in Davidson, M. and Burke, R. (eds.) *Women in Management: current research issues volume II*, London, Sage.

Vinnicombe, S. (2000) 'The position of women in management in Europe', in Davidson, M. and Burke, R. (eds.) *Women in Management: current research issues volume II*, London, Sage.

Vinnicombe, S. and Colwell, N. (1995) *The Essence of Women in Management*, Hemel Hempstead, Prentice Hall.

Wallace, M. (1989) 'Towards a collegiate approach to curriculum management in primary and middle schools', in Preedy, M. (ed.) *Approaches to Curriculum Management*, Milton Keynes, Open University Press.

Walsh, S. and Cassell, C. (1995) *A Case of Covert Discrimination: report of the Women into Management Study,* London, The Bentinck Group in association with the Women in Publishing Training Committee.

Weightman, J. (1989) 'Women in management', *Educational Management and Administration,* Vol. 17 pp.119-122.

Weindling D. and Earley, P. (1987) *Secondary Headship: the first years*, Windsor, NFER-Nelson.

Welsh Office (1995) *Statistical Directorate*, Cardiff.

White, B. (2000) 'Lessons from the careers of successful women', in Davidson, M. and Burke, R. (Eds.) *Women in Management: current research issues volume II*, London, Sage.

Whitehead M. (1997) 'Gender imbalance in applications', in *The Times Educational Supplement,* 21 November.

Wild, R. (1994), 'Barriers to women's promotion in FE', *Journal of Further and Higher Education*, 18 (3), Autumn. pp.83 – 95.

Worrall, A.M. (1995) 'Suit-able for promotion: a game of educational snakes and ladders', in Dunlap, D. and Schmuck P.A. (eds.) *Women Leading in Education*, Albany, N.Y., State University of New York Press.

Yewlett, H.L. (1996) 'Welsh Women and Educational Management', paper delivered at the BERA conference, Seville, September

Appendix

Questionnaire for Female Headteachers in England and Wales

This questionnaire was then used with minor modifications – e.g. wife/partner substituted for husband/partner – for a survey of male headteachers.

Name

Formal Qualifications

Marital Status:

Age group:

Under 30	☐
30 – 39	☐
40 – 49	☐
50 – 59	☐
60 and over	☐

School

please indicate which of the following apply to your school:

mixed	☐
11 – 16	☐
girls only	☐
11 – 18	☐
grant-maintained	☐
13 – 18	☐
LEA	☐
other age group	☐
voluntary aided	☐
voluntary controlled	☐

1. Year of appointment to present post

2. Is this your first headship?

Yes ☐ No ☐

If no please indicate the number and duration (in years) of previous headship(s)

headship one ☐ years ☐
headship two ☐ years ☐
headship three ☐ years ☐

3. Before you became a headteacher, were you a deputy head?

Yes ☐ No ☐

If so, please indicate the number and duration (in years) of deputy headship(s)

deputy headship one ☐ years ☐
deputy headship two ☐ years ☐
deputy headship three ☐ years ☐

Your main area(s) of responsibility as deputy head?

4. Please tick any of the following posts you have held:

senior teacher or equivalent ☐
head of faculty ☐
head of department ☐
post of mainly pastoral responsibility eg head of house ☐
other (please specify) ☐

5. What is your specialist subject area?

6. At what stage of your life did you formulate a career plan that included headship or deputy headship?

at school ☐
in higher education ☐
on becoming a teacher ☐
on gaining a post of responsibility ☐
never ☐
other (please specify below) ☐

7. What or who has had a major influence on your career path? (mark all those that apply)

parents ☐
partner ☐
friends ☐
your teachers ☐
domestic circumstances ☐
other (please specify below) ☐

If you are or have been married or in a permanent relationship, please answer the following questions 8 – 14. If you are single, please go to question 15

8. Number of children   their present age(s)

9. If you have children, what were/are the main methods of childcare used?

nanny ☐
childminder ☐
nursery ☐
relative (indicate which) ☐

Were/are you able to make arrangements that were satisfactory to you and your family?

Yes ☐   No ☐

Comment

Who looks/looked after your child/children when ill

10. What is your partner's job?

11. To what extent do you and your partner share domestic responsibilities eg housework, shopping, cooking, washing, organising holidays and social life? Indicate an approximate overall percentage undertaken by each of you.

myself ☐

husband /partner ☐

12. Have you ever changed your job to follow your partner?

Yes ☐ No ☐

13. Has your partner ever changed his job to follow you?

Yes ☐ No ☐

14. Have you ever operated run two separate households as a result of career commitments?

Yes ☐ No ☐

15. Have you had domestic responsibilities, such as the care of elderly relatives?

Yes ☐ No ☐

If yes please indicate nature of responsibilities

16. Have you had a career break?

Yes ☐ No ☐

If you had a career break was it for :
(Please indicate length of break)

maternity leave only ☐

longer term childcare ☐

secondment to industry ☐

secondment to obtain qualifications ☐

other (please indicate) ☐

17. If you had a career break were you able to resume your career at the same level as before the break?

Yes ☐ No ☐

18. Have you ever been aware of sexist attitudes in connection with job applications or promotion?

Yes ☐ No ☐

If so, please indicate the circumstances .

19. Have you been aware of sexist attitudes from your peers or from those you work with?

Yes ☐ No ☐

If so, please indicate the circumstances

20. Were you encouraged at any time to apply for promotion?

Yes ☐ No ☐

If so, by whom? (mark all those that apply)

partner /family ☐

colleagues at work ☐

senior managers at work ☐

headteacher ☐

other (please indicate who) ☐

21. Have you had a mentor, or role model who encouraged or inspired you?

Yes ☐ No ☐

If so, please indicate the circumstances

22. Of the interview panel that selected you as headteacher, approximately how many were men and how many were women?

Men ☐ Women ☐

23. Was there a point in your career when you thought you would not achieve headship?

Yes ☐ No ☐

If so, when and why? .

24. Do you feel that as a woman you had to 'prove your worth' in a management position?

Yes ☐ No ☐

If so, please give an example? .

25. Give three key words to describe your style of management.

26. What are the key values that you are trying to promote in your school?

27. What opportunities are there for staff to talk to you?

any time as long as you are not in a meeting ☐

any time within specified limits ☐

by appointment ☐

28. While you are in school, what proportion of your time do you spend out of your office?

under 10% ☐

between 10 – 25% ☐

between 25 – 50% ☐

between 50 – 75% ☐

29. How do you encourage all the teachers in your school to develop their careers?

mentoring ☐

role play ☐

course ☐

through appraisal ☐

other (please specify below)

30. How do you encourage female teachers in your school to develop their careers?

no special ways ☐

courses for women only ☐

mentoring programme ☐

other (please specify below) ☐

31. Why do you think that you were so successful in such a competitive field?

    through hard work   ☐

    support from others   ☐

    knowing what you wanted from life   ☐

    academic prowess   ☐

    because you are a woman   ☐

    other (please specify below)   ☐

32. As a headteacher, have you ever found it an advantage to be a woman?

    Yes   ☐   No   ☐

Please give an example .

33. Would you be prepared to be interviewed as a follow up to this questionnaire?

    Yes   ☐   No   ☐

Finally, please would you tick in the list below, those qualities that you feel apply to you:

Caring	☐	Creative	☐
intuitive	☐	aware of individual differences	☐
non-competitive	☐	tolerant	☐
subjective	☐	informal	☐
highly regulated	☐	conformist	☐
normative	☐	competitive	☐
evaluative	☐	disciplined	☐
objective	☐	formal	☐

Thank you very much for taking the time to complete this questionnaire.

Index

Affirmative action/positive
    discrimination 4, 25, 144,
    159
Androgyny 101, 104
Australia 4, 91, 145, 159

Backlash 90-1, 125
Black and Asian headteachers
    86, 88, 93, 142

Career:
    breaks 72, 75, 84
    encouragement 25-26,139
    influences on choices 17-
    18
    models/patterns 13, 28,
    153
    female model 75, 76, 77
    male model 74
    planning 15-18, 73, 75
    strategies 69-74
China 5, 97,121, 150
Confidence 30-33, 133

Deputy headship 17, 23-25
Discrimination 12, 37, 41,
    43, 44, 45, 47, 146

Eire 5
Equal opportunities 8, 10, 54,
    159
    legislation 2, 39, 41, 43,
    150

Feminism 8,10, 24, 54, 117,
    144-5, 160
Feminist research 6-7
France 5

Gatekeepers 21, 127
Gender:
    impact on role 85-6,123-
    4, 126-130, 135
    of leaders in education
    2-5
    paradigms 101-7, 154
    role stereotypes 19, 23-5,
    79, 83, 84, 159
    Geographical factors 37,
    68,147, 151
Germany 5
Governors 42, 43

Headship length of 35
Headteachers:
    age 35-6, 112
    care of dependants
    59-60
    childcare 55-9, 122
    children 51-3
    domestic responsibilities
    64-6
    marital status 50-1
    partners 63
    re-location 67-9
    subject specialism 14
    qualifications 22
Hong Kong 115, 154

Israel 4

Isolation 80, 122, 156
Leadership 1, 7, 79, 123
    delegative 108
    male 89, 97
    masculine and feminine
    100, 101
    participative 99
    resentment of women
    87-89, 96
    transformational 98-9,
    154

London 37, 38, 121, 147, 151

Male culture 58, 80-82, 91-4,
    96
Management styles:
    autocratic/directive 110,
    111, 112
    collaborative and
    participative 110, 111,
    112, 107, 108, 109, 113,
    117, 154,
    efficient 110, 111, 112
    female 98, 155
    male 97, 98
    people-oriented 110, 111,
    112, 154
    spectrum of styles 112
    values driven 110, 111,
    112
Managerialism 11, 32
Masculinities 8, 11, 126
Maternity leave 52, 53, 74-5,
    140, 144, 152
Mentors/mentoring 26-8, 80,
    140

Netherlands 5
New Zealand 4, 145
Northern Ireland 4
NPQH 22, 38

Role models 26-8, 141-3, 158

Schools:
    co-educational 36-7,
    83,121
    girls' only 5, 16, 23, 36,
    83, 121, 131-2, 141,151
    boys' only 36-7, 121
Scotland 2
Selection 38-48, 94, 146

Sexual harassment 47, 92, 93-4
Singapore 4
South Africa 5, 121
Spain 5
Stereotypes 24-5, 79-91, 94-5, 98, 125, 128, 130, 133, 157
    relating to management and leadership 84-6, 87-90, 97, 98
Support 25, 45, 130-1

Teamwork 114-5

USA 4, 22, 36, 45, 72, 88, 91, 92, 97, 114,116, 136, 158

Values 110, 111, 112, 134

Wales 2, 33
Women only courses 143
Workforce, female participation 3, 47, 49
Work/life balance 49-54, 61, 149,152, 153, 158, 160